S0-BCW-330

Reading Group Choices

*Selections for Lively
Book Discussions*

Paz & Associates

1999

© 1999 Paz & Associates
All Rights Reserved.
Published in the United States by Paz & Associates.

For further information, contact:
Donna Paz, Publisher
Mark Kaufman, Editor
Reading Group Choices
Paz & Associates
2106 Twentieth Avenue South
Nashville, TN 37212-4312

800/260-8605 — phone
615/298-9864 — fax
mkaufman@pazbookbiz.com — email

Visit our websites at:
www.readinggroupchoices.com
www.pazbookbiz.com

ISBN 0-9644876-4-0

Cover design: Mary Caprio

Printed by:
Rich Printing Company, Inc.
7131 Centennial Bl.
Nashville, TN 37209
615/350-7300

A portion of the proceeds from this publication will be used to support literacy efforts throughout the United States.

This publication is dedicated to the authors, agents, publishers, book distributors, and booksellers who bring us books that enrich our lives.

ACKNOWLEDGMENTS

This fifth edition of *Reading Group Choices* reflects greater diversity than ever, with topics on business and leadership, social issues, cultural identity, parenting, contempory history and more—in addition to an eclectic and exciting collection of fiction. What better proof that books can chage lives!

We wish to thank our publishing colleagues who continue to support this publication and bring readers quality books for group discussion:

Algonquin Books of Chapel Hill	AMACOM
Back Bay Books (Little, Brown & Co.)	Bantam Doubleday Dell
Berrett-Koehler	Crown (Random House)
Calliope Press	Charles River Press
Coulsong	Curbstone Press
Farrar, Straus & Giroux	Fithian Press (Daniel & Daniel)
HarperCollins	Harvest Books (Harcourt Brace)
Hyperion Books	Innisfree Press
Iris Editions	Jossey-Bass
Little, Brown & Co.	MacMurray & Beck
Mariner Books (Houghton Mifflin)	Milkweed Editions
New Society Publishers	Random House
Riverhead Books (Putnam Publishing Group)	Routledge
Simon & Schuster	Southern Illinois University Press
Spinsters Ink	Three Rivers Books (Random House)
University Press of New England	University of Missouri Press
Vintage Books (Random House)	William Morrow & Co.
Zoland Books	

A special thanks to our Advisory Board of readers, reading discussion group leaders and booksellers who shared their expertise and love of books to screen recommendations:

"The Compulsive Reader," Compass Rose Book Shop
Diane Leslie, Dutton's Brentwood Books
Charlene Wilson Howell, Book Group Leader
Roberta Rubin, The Book Stall at Chestnut Court
Kathy Schultenover, Davis-Kidd Booksellers
Tim Smith, Schuler Books & Music

For their assistance in creating discussion topics for several of the books in this edition, we wish to thank **Lauren Baratz-Logsted, Mary Caprio, Megan DuBois, Barbara Richards Haugen,** and **Mary Ingraham.**

In appreciation of their ongoing alliance with Paz & Associates and their efforts in producing *Reading Group Choices,* we thank Mary Caprio for her cover design, and Rich Printing Company, quality book printers since 1892.

INTRODUCTION

Last year, we surveyed several hundred book groups around the country to see what we could learn about their enormous appeal and widespread proliferation. What we learned was fascinating.

In some ways, book groups are as diverse as the books they choose to read. There are multigenerational groups, workplace groups, church groups, men's groups, and mother-daughter groups. Some will only read new hardcover releases, others only used paperbacks or books from the library. Some are only interested in fiction, others in contemporary social or political issues. Some stick to the business at hand—a lively discussion limited to the contents of the book—while others allow their conversations to drift into personal experience and more intimate sharing.

One look at the subject index of this year's edition of **Reading Group Choices**—our fifth—will tell you that, no matter your interest, there's truly something for everyone. Most prevalent are books that examine family issues and relationships, women's issues, work, and social/cultural issues like homelessness, poverty, racism, and child abuse. There are also a good number of memoirs and biographies, stories of overcoming hardship and personal triumph. And you'll find some fresh material from favorite authors like Ellen Gilchrist, Chris Bohjalian, Anita Shreve, and Sebastian Faulks.

New this year—perhaps a reflection of our hopes and fears as we approach the turn of the century—are some books about the pioneer spirit, like **The Jump-Off Creek** or **The First Lady of Dos Cacahuates**, reflections about the changing face of American culture, like **The Good Citizen** or **Global Mind Change**, and a nostalgic look at the way things were, in **Praying for Base Hits** and **Maude (1883-1993)**. There are also several books, like **Daughters of the Moon, Sisters of the Sun** and **An Intricate Weave**, that shift our focus to the needs and concerns of children and young adults, and the value of mentoring.

No matter what kind of book group you belong to, or what your motivation may be for participating, we know that **all** book groups share the love of a good book, the joy of reading, and the chance to expand and enrich their understanding of the world in which we live.

Mark Kaufman and **Donna Paz**
Nashville, Tennessee
January, 1999

CONTENTS

CONTENTS (continued)

CONTENTS (continued)

CONTENTS (continued)

THE 2,000 PERCENT SOLUTION

Authors: Donald Mitchell, Carol Coles, and Robert Metz

Publisher: AMACOM, 1999

Website: www.amanet.org

Available in:
Hardcover, 256 pages. $24.95
(ISBN 0-8144-0476-6)

Genre: Nonfiction/Business

Summary

Organizations, like people, are creatures of habit. They tend to approach problems and practices in predictable ways. This book argues that such ingrained habits, which often masquerade as efficient procedures, actually obstruct growth. *The 2,000 Percent Solution* introduces "stallbusting," a process that shows how to recognize typical stalls—the Tradition Stall, Bureaucratic Stall, Disbelief Stall, and others—and overcome them. It helps readers understand how companies habitually "think small" in order to feel comfortable and in control. However, only by learning to break certain patterns can we stride rapidly forward, solve seemingly impossible problems, and arrive at the future.

Recommended by: Norman Augustine, former CEO, Lockheed

"...Offers a visionary yet common sense way to be a victor rather than a victim in today's rapidly evolving world."

Author Biography

Donald Mitchell is chairman and CEO of Mitchell and Company, a corporate strategy and finance consulting firm. **Carol Coles** is president and COO of Mitchell and Company. Both have been quoted in *Business Week, Forbes, The New York Times,* and other publications. **Robert Metz** is a former Market Place columnist of *The New York Times,* editor of *Money Talks* and author of *CBS: Reflections in a Bloodshot Eye.*

Topics to Consider

1   What are some signs of a business having become complacent? What is the danger of complacency? Discuss some thought processes that are responsible for creating complacency within a company.

2   How do the authors explain the concept of Stallbusting? Can you think of other examples of "stalls" than those described in the book? What issues do these stalls raise and how can they best be dealt with? What stalls do you see at work in your company or business? Is the concept relevant to personal life away from work?

3   What is a 2,000 percent solution? How would you recognize one? What would be more instrumental to attaining these results—personal leadership or organizational systems? Who within the organization is best-suited to advocate the theories put forth? What support would be needed to implement the changes?

4   Identify those areas within your organization where more reading or research needs to be done. What sorts of field trips would be of the greatest benefit?

5   "Don't guide from a place of fear" is one of the concepts stressed in the book. Can you think of instances when fear has influenced any of your business practices or decisions?

6   Take the time to do some personal measurements (as outlined in chapter 9). What do these measurements reveal about how you spend your time? What kinds of changes are indicated?

7   One might assume that future best practice and theoretical best practice would be virtually the same. Elucidate the differences that exist between the two. In what ways do the solutions that arise from these practices differ?

8   What struck you and stuck with you from your reading of *The 2,000 Percent Solution*? What are the key elements to remember if you want to make these theories and techniques work for you?

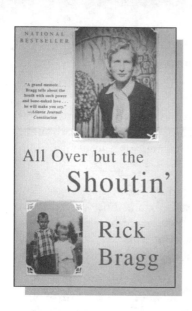

ALL OVER
BUT THE SHOUTIN'

Author: Rick Bragg

Publisher: Vintage Books
(Random House), 1998

Website: www.randomhouse.com/
vintage/read

Available in:
Paperback, 352 pages. $14.00
(ISBN 0-679-77402-5)

Genre: Nonfiction/Memoir

Summary

Rick Bragg was born in the pinewoods of Alabama to a mean-tempered, hard-drinking father and a strong-willed, loving mother, who struggled to protect her sons from the effects of poverty and ignorance that had constricted her own life. After years of abusing his wife and children, Charles Bragg abandoned the family when Rick was six. Margaret Bragg moved her three sons into her parents' house, going eighteen years without a new dress so that her children could have school clothes and working in the cotton fields so that they wouldn't have to live on welfare alone. Brash and wild like his father, Rick seemed destined for either the cotton mills or the penitentiary. Instead, he signed up for a journalism class at a nearby college. From his first job as a sportswriter for the local paper, he eventually became a Pulitzer Prize-winning reporter for *The New York Times*.

Recommended by: Pat Conroy

"...A work of art. I thought of Melville, I thought of Faulkner. Because I love the English language, I knew I was reading one of the best books I've ever read."

Author Biography

Rick Bragg, a national correspondent for the *New York Times*, earned a Pulitzer Prize for feature writing in 1996. He is based in Atlanta, Georgia.

Topics to Consider

1   Why does Bragg begin his memoir with the image of redbirds fighting? Why do you think he includes the story of a bird attacking its own image in the mirror?

2   Bragg describes a memory of himself on a gunny sack that his mother is pulling through a cotton field as she works. How does this particular image sum up his mother's love for him? Is his mother's devotion to her sons' welfare out of the ordinary?

3   Does Bragg regret his inability to forgive his dying father? Would reconciliation have alleviated Bragg's need to compensate his mother for his father's failures? What is the significance of the gift of books by an illiterate father to his clever son?

4   Did you get the impression that his memories of childhood are colored by nostalgia? To what extent do you think nostalgia plays a role in the memories and experiences of everyone?

5   Did this book change your views about the segment of society disparagingly called "poor white trash"?

6   Race relations, as Bragg shows, are complicated for poor whites in the South. What do you learn from the story of the black family down the road bringing food to Rick's mother? From his family's devotion to the demagogue George Wallace? From his work in Haiti?

7   What do you think accounts for Bragg's inability to settle down with someone? Is it a legacy from his father or simply the syndrome of a successful and driven man who doesn't have time to attend to the emotional side of life?

8   What, if any, are the definitive class barriers in our society? Does having been born poor mean that a person will always feel inferior to those who weren't?

9   Why does Bragg address one of the final chapters of his book to his father? Is he just like his father? What has he learned in the process of writing this memoir?

Editor's note: Additional topics for discussion may be found at www.randomhouse.com/vintage/read

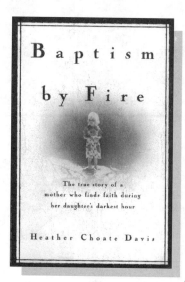

BAPTISM BY FIRE

Author: Heather Choate Davis

Publisher: Bantam Books, 1999

Website: www.bantam.com

Available in:
Paperback, 272 pages. $10.95
(ISBN 0-553-37991-7)

Genre: Nonfiction/Spirituality/Religion

Summary

Heather Davis and her husband were blessed. They had a strong and loving marriage, a terrific four-year-old son, and a new baby daughter named Remy. But one day, without warning, Remy had a seizure and was rushed to the emergency room. During the agonizing wait for her daughter's future to reveal itself, Davis learned a number of powerful lessons. She came to know the insight, grace, and compassion that strangers can offer, and discovered the depth of strength within herself and her family. Most importantly, she found a faith that would carry them through this undeniably difficult hour. This unforgettable memoir shows what happens when we open ourselves to the beauty, joy, and peace that come from faith and prayer.

Recommended by: **Marian Wright Edelman, President, Children's Defense Fund**

"This beautifully written book reminds us that while we so often struggle desperately to make everything the way we think it should be, and waste so much time on fear, God is waiting for us to let Him help and love us."

Author Biography

Heather Choate Davis wrote advertising copy, teleplays, and screenplays before turning to prose in this, her first book. She lives with her husband and two children in Mar Vista, California, where she teaches creative writing at the First Lutheran School of Venice.

Topics to Consider

1   "Promises" is the title of the first chapter. What promises did Heather Davis carry into her adult life?

2   Do you think the Episcopal church was justified in refusing to perform the baptism? What role, if any, did that denial have in Heahter's faith journey?

3   Would Heather have dealt with the crisis any differently if her faith had been with her from the beginning?

4   How would you describe the strengths and weaknesses of Lon and Heather's marriage? Do they take this spiritual journey together?

5   How did they balance the needs of their healthy child with those of their sick child? Do you think they did a good job?

6   Put yourself in Heather's place at each stage of the crisis. How would your reactions have been similar or different?

7   What role did Pastor Ken play in Heather's spiritual growth?

8   Not long before Remy's seizure, Heather avers that the world holds "no grace, no logic, no hope, no master plan." After this life-changing experience, how does she see the world? How does her use of prayer develop over the months?

9   Do you think that Heather would have found her faith without the experience of her daughter's illness? Such wrenching life episodes sometimes build faith and sometimes destroy it. What makes the difference? In this case, what do you think would have happened if Remy's surgery had not had a positive outcome?

10 Why did Heather Choate Davis write this book? How does her use of capital or lower case "g" in the word God mirror the progress of her developing belief?

THE BUFFALO TREE

Author: Adam Rapp

Publisher:
HarperCollins, 1998

Website: www.harpercollins.com

Available in:
Paperback, 192 pages. $11.00
(ISBN 0-06-440711-X)

Genre: Fiction

Summary

Clipping hoodies—stealing hood ornaments from cars—changed thirteen-year-old Sura's life. He's shipped off to Hamstock, a juvenile detention center that's worse than most, with its oppressive structure and culture of brutality which thrives there.

Sura and his patchmate, a kid named Coly Jo, look out for each other and try to evade the Stock's sadistic games. But things turn bad fast for Coly Jo, and Sura helplessly watches his friend's descent into hell, determined to escape with his own body and spirit intact—if he can. Sura relies on this inner strength—his only weapon—to keep him sane.

Recommended by: *Kirkus Reviews*

"A distinctive, compelling narrative. Rapp writes in earthy but adept language in this dark and stirring novel."

Author Biography

Adam Rapp is a playwright and novelist, whose works have been produced and developed by New York Theatre Workshop, Steppenwolf Theater Company, New York City's Public Theatre, and the Eugene O'Neill National Playwrights Conference. Mr. Rapp lives in New York City. *The Buffalo Tree* is his second novel.

Topics to Consider

1   Discuss how the language and vocabulary used by the juvies create a culture unique to Hamstock. Why do the juvies have their own language? How does Sura's language reveal his naiveté? His wisdom?

2   What role does time play in Sura's life? What sort of presence does time have in the detention center? How do you think it will affect Sura's life after he is free?

3   Consider the dead tree as a symbol in the novel. How are the classic associations with a tree—life, growth—called into question in *The Buffalo Tree?* How are they upheld? Why is the dead tree left standing?

4   Discuss Sura's relationship with Deacon Bob Fly. Is Deacon Bob Fly's attempt to help Sura sincere? Does Sura have any respect for him?

5   The novel is filled with a collection of unique character names—Slider, Dean Petty, Boo, Long Neck, and Mr. Rose. What is the significance of these and other names in the novel? Why do you think we never find out Sura's first name?

6   How is Sura affected by witnessing Coly Jo's abuse and downfall? What does Sura miss about Coly Jo?

7   What is Slider's role in Sura's life? Why is Slider's advice so important to Sura, and why does Sura trust Slider so much? Discuss Sura's relationship to Slider as a student-mentor one, and also look at Slider as a type of father figure for Sura.

8   At the end of the novel, Sura has survived his sentence at Hamstock and has returned home with his spirit and his sanity intact. What elements of juvy life remain in Sura's routine? Do you think that, in time, Sura will give up all rituals of his life at Hamstock?

9   What can we learn about the juvenile rehabilitation system from Sura's fictional story? Do you consider Coly Jo or Sura criminals? Is Sura rehabilitated? Has Hamstock rehabilitated him?

Editor's note: Additional topics for discussion may be found at www.harpercollins.com

CHARLOTTE GRAY

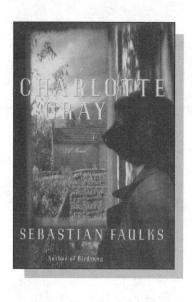

Author: Sebastian Faulks

Publisher: Random House, 1999

Website: www.randomhouse.com

Available in:
Hardcover, 416 pages, $24.95
(ISBN 0-375-50169-X)

Genre: Fiction

Summary

Similar to Faulks's previous novel, ***Birdsong***, in its wartime setting and dramatic depiction of a complex love affair that is both shaped and thwarted by war, ***Charlotte Gray*** is set in England and France during the darkest days of World War II. It is the story of a young Scottish woman who falls in love with an RAF pilot shortly before his plane is lost over France. She contrives to go there herself to work in the Resistance and also to search for him, but then is unwilling to leave as she finds that the struggle for the country's fate is intimately linked to her own battle to take control of her life.

Author Biography

Sebastian Faulks worked as a journalist before taking up writing full-time in 1991. ***Charlotte Gray*** is his third novel, following ***A Fool's Alphabet*** and the national bestseller ***Birdsong***. He lives in London with his wife and three children.

Topics to Consider

1 The author described his motivation for writing this novel in this way: "I wanted to look at the insidious way that war affects individual lives." War has an obvious affect on the love affair between Charlotte and Peter Gregory: it interrupts it. But what deeper effect does the war have on them as individuals, and how does it change the course of their relationship?

2 Shortly after meeting, Charlotte and Dick Cannerly talk about patriotism. Are people any more or less patriotic now than they were during World War II? Are wars waged to protect all that is valuable, or to fight the enemy? What values today are worth fighting for?

3 Daisy finds Gregory a bit frightening and suggests to Charlotte, "Though I suppose that's the part you've fallen for." Do you agree with Daisy's assessment? How else might you explain Charlotte's attraction?

4 Discuss the strengths and weaknesses of the relationship between Charlotte and Peter. Is their relationship based on love as you know it? On obsession? On attempts at resolving past issues?

5 When Charlotte is living in France working for the Resistance she becomes increasingly attracted to the elderly Jewish artist, Levade, and, for different reasons, to his son, Julian. What do these men represent to her, and what is she searching for in her relationship with them?

6 How does Charlotte's experience in France enable her to confront the problems of her own past and particularly the trouble between her father and herself?

7 Many reviewers have praised Faulks's strengths as an historical novelist, particularly his skill with detail and his ability to bring his period settings to life. What scenes and settings in Charlotte Gray are especially evocative as a result of his writing? Do you think that the author's attention to detail about war diminishes or enhances the love story? Do details about the relationship affect what the author has to say about war?

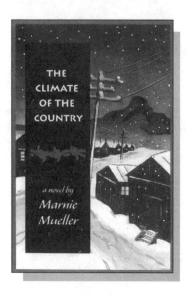

THE CLIMATE OF
THE COUNTRY

Author: Marnie Mueller

Publisher: Curbstone Press, 1999

Website: www.connix.com/~curbston/

Available in:
Hardcover, 305 pages. $24.95
(ISBN 1-880684-58-6)

Genre: Fiction/Multicultural

Summary

The Climate of the Country opens as violence erupts at the Tule Lake Japanese American Segregation Camp. The story is told from the unique insider view of Denton Jordan, a conscientious objector, and his wife Esther, living and working in the Camp. Denton is a pacifist during a time when being a man means "shouldering a gun for America," while Esther is the daughter of Jewish intellectuals actively involved in getting Jews out of Europe.

Recommended by: *Booklist*, American Library Association

"Novelist Mueller was born in the Tule Lake Camp, and her story is loosely based on her parents' experiences, but what makes this a riveting novel is not only the strong sense of history and the particulars of the racist internment but also the way the politics is played out in family, work, and erotic love."

Author Biography

Marnie Mueller is a former Peace Corps volunteer. Her first novel about her experience in Ecuador, *Green Fires*, won a Before Columbus Foundation American Book Award and a Maria Thomas Award for Outstanding Fiction. A German Translation, *Grüne Feuer*, was published in 1996 by Goldman/Bertelsmann. Craig Anderson Productions has optioned *Green Fires* for a feature film. Mueller lives with her husband in New York City.

Topics to Consider

1   What is "The Climate of the Country" the title refers to? Are there other periods in American history which the title would fit? Is there another title that would have suited the story?

2   How would you describe Denton and Esther's marriage?

3   Commitment to a person or a cause is generally regarded as a positive trait. In what ways does commitment lead to problems in this novel?

4   Auden once wrote: "I and the public know / What all school children learn. / Those to whom evil is done / Do evil in return." How does that comment fit Nebo and others in the novel?

5   Herm and Denton's friendship is nearly destroyed when Herm blames Denton for Toki's death. Where does the responsibility for Toki's death lie?

6   Why does Denton continue his affair with Alice after vowing to himself to end it?

7   Discuss Denton's character. Was he a coward or very brave?

8   Esther's grandmother plays a crucial role in her development as a person. How would you describe their relationship? Compare the advice given to Esther (p. 243) by her grandmother with Herm's advice to Denton (p. 281) never to tell Esther about his affair with Alice.

9   Do you feel that some of the conflicts in the novel are not neatly or fully resolved, and if so, do you consider it a flaw or a strength? Is the unusual connection between sex and politics rendered convincingly?

10 Differences in culture often lead to miscommunications and misunderstandings. Can you find examples of cultural insensitivity that lead to conflict? On the other hand, what are some of the common grounds of understanding in the novel?

11 Why were Japanese Americans interned but not German Americans? Do you think that most American citizens are aware of how citizens and immigrants of Japanese ancestry were treated during World War II? If not, why not?

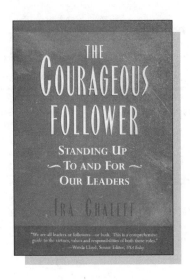

THE COURAGEOUS FOLLOWER
Standing Up To and For Our Leaders

Author: Ira Chaleff

Publisher: Berrett-Koehler, 1998

Website: www.bkpub.com

Available in:
Paperback, 212 pages. $17.95
(ISBN 1-57675-036-1)

Genre: Business/Government

Summary

Knowing how to develop strong followers, and how to be strong followers ourselves when necessary, are skills that can make or break our careers and organizations. **Ira Chaleff** presents a model for working with leaders that will forever dispel our image of followers as passive or weak. It explores the dynamics of the leader-follower relationship and offers numerous insights into how these roles partner effectively. For anyone who works closely with a leader of any kind, this book is a comprehensive guide for helping the leader use power wisely to accomplish the organization's purpose.

Recommended by: General Walter Ulmer, Jr.

"...Contains remarkable insight and a lot of practical advice that will be of enormous benefit to followers, and maybe even more benefit to leaders."

Author Biography

Ira Chaleff is president of Executive Coaching & Consulting Associates in Washington, DC (www.exc-coach.com) bringing out the full potential of senior managers and their teams. He is also chairman of the board of the Congressional Management Foundation which provides coaching and consulting services to political leaders and their staffs.

Topics to Consider

1 Did your thoughts about followers having the capacity to influence the leader-follower relationship change after reading this book? Do you think that the concept of a "courageous follower" is an oxymoron?

2 Many followers expect a great deal of their leaders. Where do these expectations have their origins? Are they realistic?

3 Does your organization have a mission statement with a clearly defined purpose? Is it compelling enough for both leaders and followers to feel loyal to that purpose?

4 Which of the sources of a follower's power (p. 16) rings most true for you personally? Which do you think is most important to cultivate?

5 If you or your family's need for security clashed with the need to risk that security for higher principles, how would you resolve this conflict?

6 For leaders and followers to embrace service to the organization as their guiding principle, what motivation is needed? When maximizing shareholders' return on investment is a dominant purpose, how is employee motivation affected?

7 Do you agree or disagree that it is acceptable to bend or break "the rules," when the enforcement of said rules would work against the organization's purpose?

8 Chapter 5 speaks to the courage to participate in transformation. What is your attitude about change? Can an "old dog learn new tricks?" Is personal change more difficult than organizational change?

9 In Chapter 5, Chaleff states that "modeling vulnerability is a real test of courage." Is this equally true for men and women? Why or why not?

10 Do you believe that it is necessary to have either witnessed or experienced transformation of some kind in order to believe in its possibility?

11 Which courageous act described in the book—assuming responsibility, serving, challenging, participating in transformation, or leaving—would be most challenging for you? Why?

DAUGHTERS OF THE MOON, SISTERS OF THE SUN

Young Women & Mentors on the Transition to Womanhood

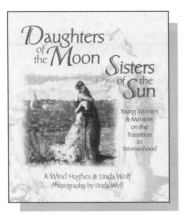

Author: K. Wind Hughes & Linda Wolf

Publisher: New Society Publishers, 1997

Website: www.newsociety.com

Available in:
Quality paperback, 240 pages. $19.95
(ISBN 0-86571-377-4)

Genre: Women's Studies/Parenting

Summary

Making the transition into womanhood is a time of great potential, discovery, and confusion. Girls often face it alone with the danger of losing their sense of self and purpose along the way. This book, a recipient of The Athena Award for excellence in mentoring, brings together girls, young women, and accomplished women mentors including poet Maya Angelou, Cherokee Chief Wilma Mankiller, The Indigo Girls rock group, author Riane Eisler, and former bionic woman Lindsay Wagner. These candid autobiographical stories offer a starting point for dialogue between girls, their parents, and caring adults about the realities that face girls today including body image, drugs, relationships, self-esteem, sex, pregnancy, race, and abuse. Includes stunning photographs, web site resources, and guidance for starting a mentoring group.

Recommended by: Rebecca Walker, author, *To Be Real*

"The women in this book...give us a glimpse of what a different and more balanced world this would be if young women's voices and dreams were heard and respected."

Author Biography

K. Wind Hughes and **Linda Wolf** are co-Directors of the Daughters/Sisters Project based on Bainbridge Island, WA. Wolf, a distinguished photographer, and Hughes, a licensed therapist, are consultants, writers, speakers and workshop leaders on girls' development, gender partnership and women's psychology.

Topics to Consider

1 This book explores many controversial and emotion-packed issues faced by teens and their parents, including teen pregnancy. Do you have a personal experience with teen mothers/fathers to share? How do you approach your teen daughters and sons about this issue?

2 Share your reactions to the girls' narratives. Which story had the most impact?

3 Riane Eisler comments that "women get disappeared in history." How does our culture's limited recognition of women as shapers of history affect us as young women?

4 As a parent who may have grown up in the '60s and '70s, how has the drug culture affected you personally and how do you approach your kids about drugs?

5 In the US, a woman is raped every six minutes and over 250,000 children, mostly girls, are molested each year. What aspects of our culture support this violence against girls and women?

6 Moral authorities, peers, the media, and the advertising industry send conflicting messages to girls about their sexuality. How do you think this affects girls' self-image?

7 Sociologists have pointed to our culture's lack of "coming-of-age" ceremonies. How might celebrating a girl's first menstruation together with other girls and older women be significant?

8 Since coming-of-age rituals are unusual in our culture, they can feel a bit awkward. Have you conducted or participated in such a ceremony before? Discuss what worked, what did not work, and ideas for future ceremonies.

9 Psychologists have written about the phenomenon of girls losing their self-esteem when they reach adolescence. Can you relate? Do you know of anyone following this pattern? How do you think we can help adolescent girls hold on to their self-esteem?

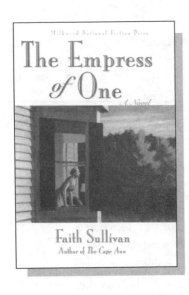

THE EMPRESS OF ONE

Author: Faith Sullivan

Publisher: Milkweed Editions, 1996

Website: www.milkweed.org

Available in:
Paperback, 416 pages. $14.95
(ISBN 1-57131-016-9)

Genre: Fiction

Summary

In this book, Faith Sullivan returns to Harvester, Minnesota, to tell the Depression-era story of Sally Wheeler and her mother, Stella. Sally is a creative child, forced to grow up amid the swirling gossip of a small town, gossip that often centers on her family. Supported by her friends (characters who also appear in *The Cape Ann*) and her own determined, sometimes destructive spirit, Sally copes with her mother's worsening mental illness and town's censure. Sally's talent and ambition as an actress and playwright allow her to find release in worlds of her own creation, where she is always an "empress of one."

Recommended by: *Rocky Mountain News*

"The novel succeeds on several levels. Sullivan has an unerring ability to capture the inner world of her characters whether they are 7 or 70."

Author Biography

"A demon gardener," (her own words), **Faith Sullivan** has lived most of her life in the midwest. She began writing novels in 1975, when yer youngest child started school, and intends to "write until her pencil runs out of lead." She is the author of four previous novels including *Repent, Lanny Merkel, Watchdog, Mrs. Demming and the Mythical Beast,* and *The Cape Ann.*

Topics to Consider

1   Faith Sullivan creates the town of Harvester with such detail that readers can imagine strolling down its streets. What words would you use to describe the town's "personality"? How, like the other characters, does Harvester grow and change over the course of the novel?

2   How does Sullivan use nostalgia to illuminate the pleasures and harsh realities of life in Harvester? Does her portrait of small town life come across as appealing or parochial?

3   Do you consider Don Wheeler a good father and husband? Given what was known at the time about mental illness, do you think he did what he could to help his wife? How does he compare with some of the other men in Harvester?

4   Why do you think Sally is drawn to Cole Barstable? Is the relationship a healthy one?

5   Sally's two grandmothers are constantly arguing over Stella's behavior. How do their personalities and relationship reflect the larger society in which Sally comes of age?

6   Sally, Lark, and Beverly all emerge as creative young women with interest in drama, literature, and fine art. How do their talents reflect their individual histories, and how is each helped by her ability to express herself creatively?

7   How does Sullivan emphasize the importance of normalcy in a town like Harvester? How many truly "normal" people do we meet in her novel? What factors do the townspeople use to judge each other?

8   What does the title, ***The Empress of One***, mean to you? What is the significance of the fairy tale, *"The Empress of One Hundred,"* and its message, "The world will have ogres, do what we may. So we must have music, sweetmeats, and play."? What does Sally's father mean when he reminds her that a good monarch is compassionate?

Editor's note: additional topics for discussion may be found at www.milkweed.org

THE FIRST LADY OF DOS CACAHUATES

Author: Harriet Rochlin

Publisher: Fithian Press, 1998

Website: www.danielpublishing.com

Available in:
Paperback, 230 pages. $11.95
(ISBN 1-56474-264-4)
Hardcover, 230 pages. $19.95
(ISBN 1-56474-265-2)

Genre: Fiction/Jewish Studies

Summary

Frieda Levie, a Jewish San Franciscan, has traded her beloved city and her father's malleable suitor for an Arizona-Sonora border outpost and freewheeling Bennie Goldson. In Dos Cacahuates, the settlement Bennie foresees as a bustling port-of-entry, Frieda suffers her share of hardships: excruciating work, floods, crime, loneliness, disillusionment, and aching adjustments to unfamiliar foods, customs, languages, and searing heat. But there are pluses as well: the exhilarating discoveries of lovemaking, new surroundings to explore, friendships to cherish, and the pride of fending for oneself. Supporting the central Jewish characters is a cast of both sexes and various ethnic and racial types who resurrect an authentic early West.

Recommended by: Norma Rosen

"[The First Lady] brings her passionate heart and her ethical intellect to this winning imbroglio of Old West Jewish adventure in a novel as impeccably crafted as it is delightful."

Author Biography

Harriet Rochlin has been researching, writing, and lecturing on Jewish roots in the West for twenty-five years. She is the author of *Pioneer Jews: A New Life in the Far West*, now in its ninth printing, and *The Reformer's Apprentice: A Novel of Old San Francisco*.

Topics to Consider

1   This novel features three types of Jewish women, as portrayed by Frieda, Minnie and Lollie. Discuss the differences between these characters. What does the author aim to achieve by putting them side-by-side?

2   Did you find the characters real? Were you moved by any of them? If this story were a movie, which part would you like to play?

3   How would this town-building story differ if told from Bennie's point of view?

4   Frieda and Bennie are strongly attracted to one another, but in upbringing, habitations, interests, and aims they're radically dissimilar. Will they be able to bridge their differences? If so, at what cost?

5   What kind of communal life can Frieda expect in her new home? What will become of the traditional practices learned at her family's kosher boardinghouse?

6   Frieda sorely misses her beloved San Francisco. What does she gain by pioneering an outpost with settlers of diverse cultures and objectives?

7   How did you react to Passover as celebrated in Dos Cacahuates? Minnie and Mendel's courtship? The scene between Frieda and Lollie at the pond?

8   Did the relationships between Mexicans, Native Americans and the newcomers along the border strike you as realistic?

9   Do you see this novel as an extension of or a departure from most fiction set in the early West?

10 Did this novel alter your understanding of western pioneers? Women in the early West? Jews in nineteenth-century America?

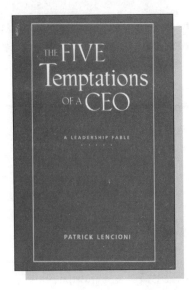

THE FIVE TEMPTATIONS
OF A CEO

Author: Patrick Lencioni

Publisher: Jossey-Bass, 1998

Website: www.josseybass.com

Available in:
Hardcover, 176 pages. $20.00
(ISBN 0-7879-4433-5)

Genre: Business/Leadership

Summary

Reminiscent of Blanchard's *One Minute Manager* and Goldratt's *The Goal, The Five Temptations of a CEO* tells the story of a young, ambitious, and overwhelmed Andrew O'Brian who, while walking to his train at the end of the day, agonizes over his year-end review with the company's board of directors the following morning. Contemplating his "decidedly unspectacular performance," he happens upon an unlikely guide in the commuter underworld who distills the seemingly infinite list of executive perils into "the five temptations of a CEO."

Recommended by: Eric Schmidt, CEO, *Novell Corporation*

"This book provides extraordinary insights into the pitfalls that leaders face when they lose sight of the true measure of success—results. Required reading for my staff."

Author Biography

Patrick Lencioni is president of The Table Group, an organizational development and consulting company. He has worked as a trainer, coach, and consultant with hundreds of executives and lives in San Francisco, California.

Topics to Consider

1   Was Andrew a sympathetic character? Did you find yourself 'pulling' for him?

2   How does Andrew compare to the average leader in your experience? About the same? Better? Worse?

3   In the book, Andrew falls to temptation number two, and then fires his marketing executive because the marketing department continued to 'fail.' Why is it difficult for people in the workplace to confront others about performance and behavioral issues?

4   Katherine is the only strong female character in the story. How might the five temptations uniquely impact women in business? In other leadership roles?

5   Which character would make the best leader?

6   How does leadership differ in the corporate world compared to other fields (coaching, politics, family, teaching, etc.)?

7   Discuss relevant methods of learning in light of temptation number three. Do people learn more when their leaders take decisive action or when they gather and present analytical information?

8   Temptation number one is placing more emphasis on status, instead of results. Focus on your own leadership roles, and ask yourself, "What is the best day of your leadership career?"

9   What do you think happened to Andrew after the Board Meeting?

10 Assess a public figure using the five temptations. Use either our current, or a former, President of the United States and determine where he overcomes, and falls, to each of the temptations.

FLIGHTS OF ANGELS

Author: Ellen Gilchrist

Publisher: Little, Brown & Co., 1998

Website: www.littlebrown.com

Available in:
Hardcover, 335 pages. $24.00
(ISBN 0-316-31486-2)

Genre: Fiction

Summary

The opening story sets the theme for this new collection: the intricate and inexorable relationships between power, love, and loss. In the ensuing stories, parents and children, siblings, and lovers tread the treacherous paths of love. The reader is treated to tales from familiar Gilchrist characters—Rhoda, and Traceleen and Crystal—and is introduced to a gallery of sparklingly eccentric new ones. Caught in the snares the heart spins, they all learn the cost and pain of love, while reveling in its joy and hilarity. The final story asserts the universal need to extend one's love beyond family and friends and to make one's mark upon the world—to improve it. In Gilchrist's world, where we encounter divorce, avarice, and death, we also find hope, laughter, and the redemption of the human heart.

Recommended by: *Chicago Tribune*

"Few pleasures can match the satisfaction of a collection of short stories by Ellen Gilchrist."

Author Biography

Ellen Gilchrist is the author of fourteen books, including *Victory Over Japan*, which won the National Book Award for fiction. She lives in Arkansas and Mississippi.

Topics to Consider

1 Think about the issues in these collected short stories. Do they mainly reflect Southern history and culture, or could these stories take place anywhere?

2 How are the issues of race and sex intertwined in "A Tree To Be Desired" and in many of the other stories in this collection? How are Juliet and the other women in these stories treated by the men they married?

3 "A Lady With Pearls" continues the theme of the divide that often exists between husband and wife. In this and other stories collected here, the husbands are unfaithful and the wives unhappy. There is very little contentment. What is Gilchrist saying about the state of marriage?

4 Why did the author title the book *Flights of Angels*? Who are the angels she refers to?

5 Discuss the differing attitudes about family depicted throughout this collection. Is there a "typical Southern family" in these pages? Do you share the author's view of family or do you see family in another light?

6 Rhoda and Abby leave on a weekend trip to starve themselves, drink and kill time. The irony of the problems they leave at home with Rhoda's children are made clear when they are called back to see to the LSD that Rhoda's son has slipped with his friend, and the adults stay up late drinking gin while talking about the boy's problems. Discuss the pre-recovery era of overlapping values, between the sexual revolution, prescription drugs and the drug culture. Is drinking any different from taking drugs? If so, how? How do adults and teenagers differ in their answers to these questions?

7 In "Miss Crystal Confronts the Past" and "A Sordid Tale, or, Traceleen Continues Talking", is Traceleen's race particularly relevant to the telling of these stories about Crystal? If so, why?

8 In "Phyladda, or, The Mind/Body Problem" Jodie rediscovers the power of good deeds. Is this a power that you believe in? Have you ever had an experience like Jodie's?

GLOBAL MIND CHANGE
The Promise of the 21st Century

Author: Willis Harman

Publisher: Berrett-Koehler, 1998

Website: www.bkpub.com

Available in:
Paperback, 226 pages. $17.95
(ISBN 1-57675-029-9)

Genre: Nonfiction/Social Issues

Summary

In this book, **Willis Harman** reveals that, in fact, we are living through one of the most fundamental shifts in history—a change in the actual belief structure of Western industrial society. He shows how this shift, manifest in five major areas of human concern—science and education, spirituality and consciousness research, health and healing, psychology and psychotherapy, and economics and management—is revolutionizing education, altering the way we interpret science, facilitating major changes in business and finance, and forcing us to rethink policies of national and global security.

Recommended by: Roger Walsh, MD, *University of California*

"...This book sparkles with a host of provocative ideas for working with the far-reaching changes that we, our culture, and our planet now face."

Author Biography

Willis Harman, Ph.D., was a prolific author, influential social thinker and futurist, scientist, businessman, and educator. He was a founding board member of the World Business Academy and served as president of the Institute of Noetic Sciences for almost twenty years. He died in 1997.

Topics to Consider

1 Harman discusses how several scientific discoveries have caused "profound shock" throughout time. One example is Galileo's findings that the Earth is not the center of the universe. What other revelations have taken place during the last century that similarly affected our collective understanding?

2 Meditation and certain other elements of Eastern medicine are taken more seriously by Western medical professionals today than they were in the past. How has public interest in alternative medicine affected the medical community? In what other areas of Western culture do you see similar shifts taking place?

3 Harman points out that the "mind over matter" view is increasingly accepted by business and health care professionals. Does your own experience agree with Harman's perceptions?

4 Maslow observed that "we are all ambivalent when it comes to knowing ourselves" and that Western culture has taught us not to trust ourselves. Have you encountered these messages during your lifetime? If so, describe the circumstances. Have your beliefs changed over time?

5 Discuss Harman's statement that bigness and concentration of power are among the chief contributors to feelings of alienation and depersonalization in modern society. Is anything gained if a "Western industrial monoculture" develops? What is lost? What forces may likely intercede in this process?

6 Four challenges to the present order are outlined on pages 150-151. Discuss any organizations or individuals who are taking leadership positions with regard to these issues today.

7 If changes in thinking take place as Harman suggests, what words would we use to describe the Earth's inhabitants, assuming that the term "consumer" would no longer be relevant?

8 Harman believes that a vast number of people would "risk destruction of civilization rather than risk fundamentally changing their perceptions of the world." If fundamental change is to take place, how do you think the process will unfold? In what time frame?

THE GOOD CITIZEN

Editors: David Batstone and Eduardo Mendieta

Publisher: Routledge, 1999

Website: www.routledge-ny.com

Available in:
Hardcover, 144 pages. $21.00
(ISBN 0-415-92093-0)

Genre: Nonfiction/
Current Affairs/Politics

Summary

In *The Good Citizen*, some of the most eminent contemporary thinkers take up the question of the future of American democracy in an age of globalization, growing civic apathy, corporate unaccountability, and purported fragmentation of the American common identity by identity politics. The collection shows that American democracy has been and continues to be full of possibilities because its culture of citizenship has been a creative and nurturing space for new citizens to make their claims on civil, political and social justice. The contributors stand for the affirmation of both cultural identity and a common civic culture and call for political accountability and participation.

Author Biography

David Batstone and **Eduardo Mendieta** teach at the University of San Francisco. Batstone is author of *New Visions for the Americas* and *From Conquest to Struggle.* Mendieta is the editor of *Latin America and Postmodernity* and *Ethics and the Theory of Rationality.* They are co-editors of *Liberation Theologies, Postmodernity and the Americas* (Routledge 1997).

Topics to Consider

1   What does it mean to be an American? Why has this question become code language for a conversation about race relations in the USA?

2   "America is a melting pot." Do you react positively or negatively to this characterization of our cultural heritage?

3   Why do you think such a large majority of U.S. citizens say they have lost confidence in our public institutions' ability to lead? "Question Everything," goes the bumper sticker. Is that a healthy development or does it portend a crisis for our democratic style of government?

4   Is patriotism a civic virtue or chauvinistic nationalism?

5   Are citizens morally bound to honor a social contract that binds them to their "fellow citizens"?

6   In a democracy, should the government be empowered to intervene in the promotion of social ideals, such as equal opportunity for all citizens? Or is the primary purpose of the government to ensure fundamental rights of privacy and ownership?

7   How has the rise of multinationalism challenged our traditional sense of being an American?

8   What is the relationship between religion and citizenship? Are they mutually exclusive or do they enable each other?

9   The United States is founded on a history of immigration. So why do certain groups still lack full economic, social, and political integration? Is citizenship something that we refuse to certain groups, despite our historical rhetoric? If so, why?

10 What will happen to "race politics" in the 21st century, when today's racial "minorities" will no longer be in the minority? Latinos, and Asian-Americans, an equally heterogeneous group of people, will be the dominant "minorities" in the 21st century U.S. How will this change the racial grammar of American politics?

A GRACIOUS PLENTY

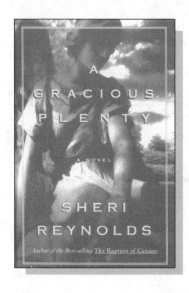

Author: Sheri Reynolds

Publisher: Three Rivers Press
(Random House), 1999

Website: www.randomhouse.com

Available in:
Paperback, 208 pages. $12.00
(ISBN 0-609-80387-5)

Genre: Fiction

Summary

In the lush and isolated cemetery of a small Southern town, Finch Nobles tends to the flowers and shrubs that surround the monuments of people who were not known to her while they lived but who in death have become her lifeline. Badly burned in a household accident when she was just four, Finch grows into a courageous and feisty loner. She eschews the pity and awkward stares of the people of her hometown and discovers that if she listens closely enough, she can hear the voices of those who have gone before. Finally, when she speaks, they answer back telling their stories in a chorus of regrets, explanations, and insights.

Recommended by: *Publishers Weekly*

"Reynolds's lyricism and the gentle voice of her heroine carry this poignant but redemptive story of an emotionally and physically scarred woman who finds her way out of the land of the dead and into the land of the being."

Author Biography

Sheri Reynolds teaches writing and literature at Old Dominion University. She is a native of South Carolina, a graduate of Davidson College and Virginia Commonwealth University, and lives now in Norfolk, Virginia. Her previous novels are ***Bitterroot Landing*** and ***The Rapture of Canaan***.

Topics to Consider

1   As a child, Finch tries to hide her scarred face. How do her parents' reactions to her scars affect her own?

2   Does Finch's acceptance of her scars parallel the freedom that comes with the Dead's letting go of secrets and burdens?

3   Is Finch's "harassment" of Lucy's mother justifiable? Do the requests of the Dead take precedence over the needs of the living to protect themselves?

4   As Lucy suggests, Is Finch herself guilty of judging people by appearances and superficial behavior?

5   When the group of teenage girls misbehaves in the cemetery (p. 77), Finch relates the stories of the people buried in various graves. Why do the stories make the girls less fearful? How does the incident mark a change in Finch's attitude toward the living?

6   When Finch asks for Leonard's father as a lawyer when she is arrested for harassing Lucy's mother, Mr. Livingston immediately begins denigrating his son. What do his actions tell you about the scars Leonard bears? Are they as damaging as the scars Finch has had to cope with?

7   As William conjures up the storm to avenge the desecration of his grave, Finch's father and the Mediator warn Finch to leave the cemetery. Why is Finch so reluctant to go, even though the cemetery feels like a strange place to her for the first time?

8   How accurate is Leonard's accusation that Finch cut herself off from people because she feared they would mistreat her? (p. 169) Does her isolation and her often provocative behavior belie her constant declarations that she fully accepts her disfigurement?

9   Throughout the novel, the Dead display all the characteristics of the living—they whine, they argue, they express anger and seethe with jealousy and resentment. How did this vision of life after death affect you? How would you reconcile Reynolds's description with more traditional religious views?

GYPSY DAVEY

Author: Chris Lynch

Publisher: HarperCollins, 1998

Website: www.harpercollins.com

Available in:
Paperback, 180 pages. $11.00
(ISBN 0-06-440730-6)

Genre: Fiction

Summary

By age twelve, Davey has had his share of problems. For his entire existence he has lived with a mother who loves him, but refuses to learn how to be a parent to him; a charismatic but reckless father who can't seem to commit to his family; and a sister, Joanne, who had to become his real mother when she was seven years old. Alternately adored and abused by his older sister, Davey grows up with the passionate conviction that somehow his life should be better than it is. And when Joanne, now a seventeen-year-old mother herself, seems destined to repeat the mistakes of their mother with her newborn son, Davey is determined to do everything he can to spare his nephew from the harsh, desperate, and lonely childhood he himself has had.

Recommended by: *Washington Post*

"There is nothing conventional about Lynch's third and best novel. This tight, taut novel bounces back between slow-witted Davey's thoughts and his family's sad history. Oddly refreshing."

Author Biography

Chris Lynch is the author of several award-winning novels. He divides his time between working on new projects and mentoring aspiring writers.

Topics to Consider

1   Do you think that Davey has the potential to break the pattern of abuse in his family, and will treat a child differently than Lois and Joanne have? From whom does Davey learn to be so caring and loving? Would Davey be a good father?

2   Davey has several means of temporary escape from his problems, like his bike and television. Do these distractions allow Jo and Lois to escape from their responsibilities? Is escape good?

3   How and when do Jo and Lois express their love for Davey? What do other characters in the novel think of Davey? What kind of impression does Davey give?

4   What is the nature of Davey's relationship to Lester—the streetwise drug dealer who nicknames him Gypsy Davey?

5   Why is it appropriate that Davey is the photographer at Joanne's wedding? What is the significance of Davey's watching the wedding through a camera lens? What do you make of Joanne's and Lois's numerous requests to have their picture taken?

6   From reading the book, you know that Davey is a loner. But is he the loneliest character in the story?

7   Throughout the novel, abusive occurrences are narrated in the same tone as the sporadic signs of a more traditional, caring parenthood. Is abuse somehow intertwined with love for Davey?

8   How does Jo's method of raising her baby differ from Lois's? How does Jo's treatment of her baby differ from her treatment of Davey? Do these two characters treat Davey in the same way? How do the characters of Jo and Lois allow the author to comment on the issues of abuse and neglect?

9   Discuss the significance of Davey's nickname. Is Davey a gypsy? Does the significance of the nickname change as the novel progresses?

Editor's note: Additional topics for discussion may be found at www.harpercollins.com

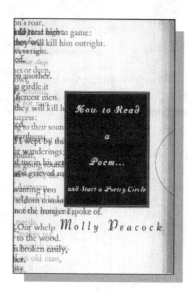

HOW TO READ A POEM...
And Start a Poetry Circle

Author: Molly Peacock

Publisher: Riverhead Books, 1999

Website: www.penguinputnam.com

Available in:
Hardcover, 144 pages. $21.95
(ISBN 1-57322-128-7)

Genre: Nonfiction/Poetry

Summary

Molly Peacock shows us why poetry begs to be shared, to be read aloud, discussed, and enjoyed among friends. *How to Read a Poem* is a slender book of ways to explore the romance we have with words we can't quite hold. In twelve chapters, Peacock presents eighteen "talisman" poems—cherished poems that she has collected over the years. Each chapter examines the interior life of both the poem and the poet, giving readers a window to their interior lives as well. *How to Read a Poem* also offers a practical and anecdotal guide to organizing a poetry reading group and a final chapter in which twenty poets present their suggestions of favorite books with which to begin your poetry reading experience.

Recommended by: The Washington Post

"Whatever the subject, rich music follows the tap of Molly Peacock's baton."

Author Biography

Molly Peacock is the president emerita of the Poetry Society of America and one of the creators of the "Poetry in Motion" series that has put poetry on the nation's subways and buses. She is the author of four books of poetry and a memoir, *Paradise, Piece by Piece.* She lives in New York City and London, Ontario.

Topics to Consider

1 Molly Peacock manages to explicate a poem without "tearing the wings" off of it. Has reading her book changed the way you approach poetry?

2 Why a poetry circle and not a poetry group? What is significant about the distinction?

3 What are the differences between a poetry circle and a reading group? How might a book group benefit from including poetry?

4 Peacock outlines three types of poetry circles—a ready made circle, a slip-in circle and a seasonal circle. Which appeals to you most? Why?

5 Do you have a "family" of poems? What do they mean to you? Which, if any, of Molly Peacock's talisman poems speak to you? What questions did Peacock ask of these poems before granting them importance? What questions would you ask of a poem before it gains importance in your life?

6 Peacock describes the three systems at work in poetry—the line, the sentence and the image—and likens them to music, story-telling and painting. Apply these systems to a poem. Do you hear the music in the line and glean the story from the sentence? Compare poetry to prose. How do the tools employed, the patterning, and the music differ between the two?

7 As Peacock suggests, it is too daunting a task to discuss an entire volume of poems at one sitting. With this in mind, choose one or two of her talisman poems for more in-depth discussion.

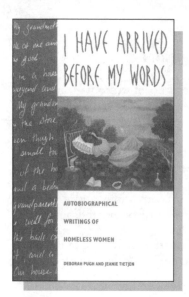

I HAVE ARRIVED BEFORE MY WORDS
Autobiographical Writings of Homeless Women

Authors: Deborah Pugh & Jeanie Tietjen

Publisher: Charles River Press, 1998

Available in:
Paperback, 210 pages. $14.00
(ISBN 0-9647124-2-3)

Genre: Nonfiction/
Memoirs/Social Issues

Summary

Most readers are familiar with homelessness as an issue and have probably passed homeless people on the street. But what are these people's lives really like? How did they become homeless? Where do they find joy? What are they like as individuals beyond the label of "homeless"? This book allows five homeless women to tell their own stories in their own words, as well as revealing the impact they had on two writing teachers who encouraged them to write and then gathered their stories in what the *Washington Post* called "a stirring and illuminating collection."

Recommended by: **Jane Alexander, Former Chairman, National Endowment for the Arts**

"This is a great story—or rather seven great stories, those of two dedicated teachers and five dedicated students, homeless women who found new voices and new lives thanks to the power of writing."

Author Biography

Deborah Pugh and **Jeanie Tietjen** met each other and their students while teaching writing with the WritersCorps program in Washington, D.C. Both have taught writing at the university level as well as in such settings as homeless shelters, jails, and senior centers. Pugh now lives in Durham, North Carolina, and Tietjen in Amherst, Massachusetts.

Topics to Consider

1   How would you describe the relationship among the seven women in this book? How do the editors' short essays on each homeless woman relate to the story each tells about herself?

2   Many definitions of home and degrees of homelessness are explored here—from the lack of a physical space of one's own to the emotional anguish of rootlessness to the spiritual quest for one's place in the world. To which of the seven women do the different definitions seem to apply? Which definitions, if any, can you relate to in your own life? Does the concept of home have an especially rich meaning for women?

3   Debbie and Jeanie speak of the community of writers they formed with the homeless women in their classes. What helped them establish those communities? How did writing together serve as a bridge?

4   Were you surprised that the homeless women's stories included incidents of both personal trauma (breast cancer, sexual abuse, addiction, mental illness) and personal happiness (giving birth, religious beliefs, cooking, friendship)? Why or why not? How is each using creativity to make her life better?

5   Gayle, Ann, Georgia, Dionne, and Angie have very distinctive writing styles. How would you characterize each? What does each woman's writing style reveal about her?

6   Why did Gayle, Angie, and Georgia become homeless? What is helping them move out of homelessness?

7   Jeanie says that writing "begs not only a concentration on the rich inner climate, but exercises an ability to envision things as they once were—or have never been but could be." How does this statement relate to all women, homeless or not, who tell their own stories? Why do some say there is both a personal and a political dimension to telling one's own story as opposed to someone else telling it?

8   Do you know anyone who has been homeless or had other life experiences similar to those described in this book? How would you compare and contrast their stories?

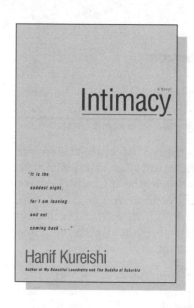

"It is the
saddest night,
for I am leaving
and not
coming back . . ."

Hanif Kureishi

Author of My Beautiful Laundrette and The Buddha of Suburbia

INTIMACY

Author: Hanif Kureishi

Publisher: Scribner, 1999

Website: www.SimonSays.com

Available in:
Hardcover, 128 pages. $16.00
(ISBN 0-684-85275-6)

Genre: Fiction

Summary

Intimacy is an exploration of the fears and desires that drive men to leave women. Kureishi's counter-hero is a father of two boys preparing to abandon the children and their mother. His departure will not be impulsive. He and Susan live comfortably in London, and though each loves the children dearly, their own intimacy has withered. No one is at fault; it has simply happened. There is much about Susan that Jay admires, and he does not seek to excuse his own behavior. Nevertheless, "contemplating this rupture from all angles," he decides to go.

Recommended by: *Time Out* (London)

"In less than 120 pages, Kureishi manages to say more than most writers at twice the length. His anger and desire to shock are still present but they are now harnessed to a new-found compassion and vision."

Author Biography

Hanif Kureishi, renowned worldwide for his screenplays *My Beautiful Laundrette* and *Sammy and Rosie Get Laid,* is also author of ***The Buddha of Suburbia*** and ***Love in a Blue Time.*** He lives in London, England.

Topics to Consider

1   Discuss the tone of Jay's narrative. How did it affect the way you perceived his story and his character? How would your reaction to Jay differ if he'd been less lucid and rational?

2   At its heart, what do you think this book is really about? Love? The disintegration of love? Boredom? Where is the intimacy to which the title refers?

3   Jay describes a childhood spent covering his ears as his parents fought, dreaming of running away forever. Do you see his abandonment of his family as an inevitable result of his childhood?

4   Is it better to endure a childhood in an unhappy, yet intact family or with parents who split up? What is more important: remaining loyal to your own needs, or to the needs of your family as a whole? Is it possible to do both when the relationship between parents disintegrates? Can one abandon his family and still be a good person?

5   Has Jay really fallen out of love with Susan, or is he depressed by the lack of excitement between them? Is he bored with her, or bored with himself? Do you think that all long-term relationships become less passionate as time goes on?

6   Why is Jay so afraid to be left alone with his own thoughts? Is Susan's need for order and organization her way of distracting herself from her problems?

7   Would reactions to this book differ between men and women? Would men have more compassion for Jay? How would this story change if Susan were the one who wanted to leave?

8   Is Jay's final night at home a secret "test" he's giving Susan to prove to him why he should stay?

9   Jay says, "Why do people who are good at families have to be smug and assume it is the only way to live?" (p. 32) What would you have to say to him in response?

10 Ultimately, is this book an argument for why Jay should stay or why he should leave?

AN INTRICATE WEAVE
Women Write About Girls and Girlhood

Editor: Marlene Miller

Publisher: Iris Editions, 1997

Available in:
Paperback, 384 pages. $15.95
(ISBN 0-945372-15-9)

Genre: Literature/
Women's Studies/Young Adults

Summary

The vibrant voices of over sixty authors give us stories, essays and poems connecting women, young women and girls through the generations. This is an inspiring and fascinating collection that readers love to share. An excellent choice for writing groups as well as book groups. *An Intricate Weave* has been warmly received by adult readers and has also been nominated as one of the Best Books for Young Adults by the American Library Association, making it particularly suitable for mother-daughter groups.

Recommended by: Kate Fitzsimmons, *San Francisco Review*

"After reading most of these pieces I found myself wanting to do two things: stop and savor the complexity of images and feelings created by these gifted women, and then call a friend and read a story aloud."

Author Biography

Marlene Miller is a writer, editor and publisher of the literary small press Iris Editions. Contributors to this anthology include such distinguished names as Julia Alvarez, Lucille Clifton, Ursula Le Guin, Faye Moskowitz, Peggy Orenstein, Adrienne Rich and Alice Walker, along with many other gifted writers. The introduction is by Kristen Golden, co-author of *Remarkable Women of the Twentieth Century*.

Topics to Consider

1 Looking back on your own youth, did you identify with any of the characters and situations in the book?

2 Was there anything different from your own growing up that you found interesting to read about?

3 What are some of the issues that girls today face? How did certain writers invite us to understand these issues more deeply?

4 Does the world of today's girls have a connection to girlhoods of the past? What are some of the similarities?

5 A number of the authors in the book write about mother and daughter relationships. Did any of the portrayals seem particularly meaningful to you?

6 Friendship is also a theme that runs through the collection. Discuss some of the varied forms that friendship takes in the works.

7 As girlhood progresses it becomes a time of dawning sexual awareness. How do the works present some of the complex realities?

8 Many of the pieces explore the role that memory plays as the authors recall their youth. How does the girl remain an important part of the adult woman?

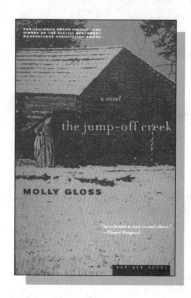

THE JUMP-OFF CREEK

Author: Molly Gloss

Publisher: Mariner Books, 1998

Website: www.hmco.com

Available in:
Paperback, 186 pages. $12.00
(ISBN 0-395-92501-0)

Genre: Fiction

Summary

The Jump-Off Creek is a full-length portrait of Lydia Sanderson, a pioneer woman who confronts and conquers the demands of homesteading alone in northeast Oregon's Blue Mountains in the 1890s. She carves a self-reliant life out of an unforgiving wilderness, arriving at Jump-Off Creek with two mules, two goats, and only those possessions that the mules can carry. In alternating entries from Lydia's journal and narrative chapters of shifting perspective, **Molly Gloss** chronicles Lydia's first nine months on her dearly purchased high-mountain homestead and her relationships with the denizens of the hardscrabble mountains. As we learn that women did clear trees and drive cattle—and men did cook and do laundry—all of our stereotypes of the West and the frontier are dispelled.

Recommended by: *Philadelphia Inquirer*

"A rare treat to find characters we can care about this much."

Author Biography

Molly Gloss is the author of many short stories and a novel for young adults, *Outside the Gates,* published both here and abroad. Her third novel, *The Dazzle of Day,* was a *New York Times* Notable Book of 1997. Gloss lives in Portland, Oregon with her husband and son and hikes the same Blue Mountain trails blazed by her pioneer forebears.

Topics to Consider

1 What is the significance of the name Jump-Off Creek for Lydia and the earlier pioneer women with whom she feels kinship?

2 Lydia tells Blue Odell that "I was seeking the boundless possibilities that are said to live on the frontier." What do you think she had in mind?

3 When confronted with difficulty or danger, in what ways does Lydia's habit of "going quick" — before the misgiving would set in — serve her well, or not?

4 Evelyn Walker's reflections on her own loneliness triggers a similar unspoken response on Lydia's part. How does Lydia deal with being alone?

5 How does each woman in the story cope with the challenges of living as a woman, single or married, on the frontier? Are there any parallels to women's lives a century later?

6 What are some of the hardships endured by Lydia and the others that require both tenderness and an absence of pity?

7 Lydia sets a high value on Tim and Blue's house being "well-established and soundly built." What else can we infer about what Lydia values?

8 In her first journal entry at Jump-Off Creek, Lydia writes, "I have not lost Heart, having done so in years past and no false hopes this time. There are Graces at all events." What are the "Graces" to which she refers?

9 What was the biggest surprise or challenge to a preconception you might have had about frontier homesteading?

Editor's note: Additional topics for discussion may be found at www.hmco.com

THE LAKE DREAMS THE SKY

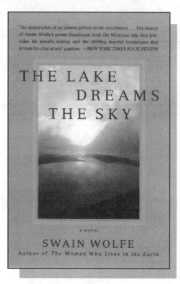

"An exploration of an almost primal erotic attachment . . . The beauty of Swain Wolfe's prose illuminates both the Montana lake that provides his novel's setting and the shifting interior landscapes that arouse his characters' passion. —*NEW YORK TIMES BOOK REVIEW*

THE LAKE
DREAMS
THE SKY

A NOVEL

SWAIN WOLFE
Author of *The Woman Who Lives in the Earth*

Author: Swain Wolfe

Publisher: Cliff Street Books (HarperCollins), 1996

Website: www.harpercollins.com/readers

Available in: Paperback, 334 pages. $13.00 (ISBN 0-06-092993-6)

Genre: Fiction

Summary

After 23 years away, Liz, a Boston businesswoman, returns to visit her eccentric grandmother and to seek solace by the lake that made her believe the world was alive and aware. Among her long-stored treasures, she uncovers a primitive painting of a woman that she connects to a legend from her childhood, a romance about a love whose passion sets the lake on fire. This novel tells the story of that post-World War II romance between Rose, a local waitress, and a drifter named Cody—lovers whose defiance of society's unwritten rules makes them outlaws in an unforgiving time.

Recommended by: Sandra Scofield

"*An irresistible novel about the pleasures of falling in love, the tensile bond between women of kin, and the pain of discovering just what it means to be an outlaw, just how dangerous it is to break the rules.*"

Author Biography

Raised on ranches in the high country of Colorado and Montana, **Swain Wolfe** has been a logger, an underground miner, and a documentary filmmaker. His previous novel is ***The Woman Who Lives in the Earth***. He lives in Montana.

Topics to Consider

1   Liz returns to the lake she grew up on. What does "returning home" mean to people? How does the experience of nature in childhood differ from what we experience as adults?

2   Throughout the novel, the theme of the relationship between primitive man and nature emerges. Primitive man spoke to nature to negotiate for more control. How has our lack of dependence on nature affected the way we view the world and one another?

3   How would the belief that the world is alive and aware change our sense of place in the world?

4   When Liz asks Ana to define romance, the old woman responds "Shared yearning." Do you agree? How would you describe romantic love?

5   Primitive man approached nature with rapture and awe. Does love today have the power and mystery that our ancestors found in nature?

6   In considering the difference between Indians and white culture, Liz says, "It's ironic that the Indians felt betrayed because their hearts weren't hardened and we feel betrayed because ours are." (p. 185) How does this reflect the relationship between Native Americans and the rest of our society?

7   In the novel, Katherine, the old Indian woman who raised Rose, embodies tradition and wisdom. Are we as aware of patterns and cycles now? How does wisdom differ in today's world?

8   Cody and Rose were ostracized in the forties because they defied society's sense of propriety. What qualities make people outlaws throughout history? Why are outlaws appealing?

Editor's note: Additional topics for discussion may be found at www.harpercollins.com/readers

THE LAW OF SIMILARS

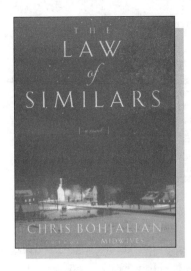

Author: Chris Bohjalian

Publisher: Harmony Books, 1999

Website: www.randomhouse.com

Available in:
Hardcover, 275 pages. $23.00
(ISBN 0-517-70586-9)

Genre: Fiction

Summary

After his wife's death in a car accident, Leland Fowler devotes himself entirely to raising his small daughter, Abby, and to his job as a Chief Deputy State's Attorney in Vermont. As the strain of daily life takes its toll, Leland seeks the help of homeopath Carissa Lake for a chronic sore throat impervious to conventional medical treatment. Carissa provides a cure not only for his sore throat, but for the aching loneliness that lies at the root of his symptoms. Leland then learns that one of Carissa's patients has fallen into an allergy-induced coma and the patient's wife has accused Carissa of having suggested a dangerous treatment for her husband's asthma. As the investigation gears up, Leland finds himself in the center of controversy, face-to-face with moral and ethical dilemmas of enormous proportions.

Author Biography

Chris Bohjalian is the author of six novels and a columnist for the *Burlington Free Press*. His most recent novel, ***Midwives***, was one of *Publishers Weekly's* Best Books of the Year, and is currently being made into an ABC-TV movie starring Jessica Lange. ***Midwives*** was also featured in the 1997 edition of ***Reading Group Choices***, and was recently named an Oprah Book Club selection. Bohjalian lives in Lincoln, Vermont, with his wife and daughter.

Topics to Consider

1   In what ways do the disciplines of psychology and homeopathy reinforce each other in Carissa's treatment of her patients? Does the success of Leland's cure depend on his willingness to trust Carissa?

2   Do you think that Richard Emmons's fear of the long-term effects of conventional medicine is realistic? Does Jennifer too willingly accept the authority of the medical establishment?

3   Is it wrong for Leland to put his feelings for Carissa above what he knows he should do as a lawyer? Discuss the distinction he makes between the ethical thing to do and the moral thing to do.

4   At what point does Leland cross the line between the commitment to upholding the law and his commitment to Carissa?

5   Why does Carissa agree to doctor her notes on treating Richard? Would you have taken Leland's advice? Do you think that Carissa's ultimate decision to leave the United States was the only one she could have made in order to live as she wanted to?

6   Each chapter is introduced with a quotation from the works of Dr. Samuel Hahnemann, the founder of homeopathy. How do they add to your understanding of the book?

7   What is the significance of Leland's increasing dependence on the arsenic pills he takes from Carissa's office? How do his reactions over the course of the novel—from his initial exhilaration to the unpleasant physical symptoms and fears he suffers at the end—relate to the law of similars that informs homeopathy?

8   When **Midwives** was first published, it led to an often heated debate about the literal and metaphoric place of birth in our culture. Do you think **The Law of Similars** will stimulate an equally earnest discussion about the role alternative medicine should play in health care?

9   Chris Bohjalian has said that **The Law of Similars** is about forgiveness. How successful are the three main characters Leland, Carissa, and Jennifer at forgiving themselves and each other?

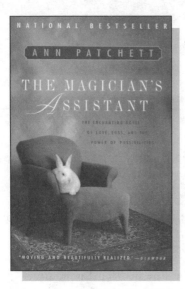

THE MAGICIAN'S ASSISTANT

Author: Ann Patchett

Publisher: Harvest
(Harcourt Brace), 1998

Website:
www.harcourtbrace.com

Available in:
Paperback, 368 pages. $13.00
(ISBN 0-15-600621-9)

Genre: Fiction

Summary

When Parsifal, a handsome and charming magician, dies suddenly, his widow Sabine—who was also his faithful assistant for twenty years—learns that the family he claimed to have lost in a tragic accident is very much alive and well. Sabine is left to unravel his secrets, and the adventure she embarks upon, from sunny Los Angeles to the bitter windswept plains of Nebraska, will work its own magic on her. Sabine's extraordinary tale will capture the heart of its readers just as Sabine herself is captured by her quest.

Recommended by: *San Francisco Chronicle*

"...The magic [Patchett] creates in this enchanting novel is of the alchemical kind—it transmutes baser elements into gold and changes everything irrevocably."

Author Biography

Ann Patchett is the author of two previous novels, *The Patron Saint of Liars*, which was a *New York Times* Notable Book of the Year, and *Taft*, which won the Janet Heidinger Kafka Prize. She has written for many publications, including *Elle*, *GQ*, *The Paris Review*, and *Vogue*. Though she now lives in Nashville, Tennessee, readers will not be surprised to discover that Los Angeles is Patchett's hometown.

Topics to Consider

1   Was Sabine genuinely happy with Parsifal? Is it possible to be happy in a marriage without passionate love? Do you think finding your true love is destiny or luck?

2   Was the illusion Parsifal created about his past understandable? Had he been born and raised in a place other than a conservative Midwestern town, would his illusion have been necessary?

3   Why do you think Sabine was able to have such a good relationship with Phan, her husband's lover, when he was alive?

4   When the airplane is struck by violent turbulence on Sabine's flight to Nebraska, she thinks dying wouldn't be so terrible. Do you think Sabine really wants to die?

5   The first magic trick that Sabine performs in Nebraska is when she pulls an egg out from behind Dot's ear. What is significant about her doing this trick at this very moment? In performing more and more magic tricks, is Sabine discovering something about her own ability, or is she simply carrying on for Parsifal?

6   Sabine watches the Johnny Carson video twice with Dot's family. Describe how her reactions differ the first and second times she watches it.

7   Do you think that Sabine and Kitty would have fallen in love had each of them not loved Parsifal? If Howard had been a better husband and father? Since Sabine and Kitty both dream of Parsifal, are we supposed to think that Parsifal has somehow brought them together?

8   At Bertie's wedding, Sabine does Parsifal's card trick from her dream. Is there a secret to this trick or is it really "magic"?

9   The book begins, "Parsifal is dead. That is the end of the story." Is Parsifal's death really the end of the story? In her last dream, Sabine waves goodbye to him. Do you think she will dream about Parsifal again? Do you think Kitty will finally leave Howard and go to Los Angeles with Sabine?

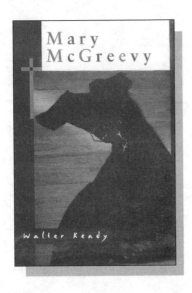

MARY McGREEVY

Author: Walter Keady

Publisher:
MacMurray & Beck, 1998

Website: www.macmurraybeck.com

Available in:
Hardcover, 263 pages. $24.00
(ISBN 1-878448-83-8)

Genre: Fiction

Summary

After her father's death, Sister Mary Thomas leaves her convent to reclaim the family farm in the Irish village of Kildawree. In 1950, her status as ex-nun scandalizes the women of the village, but her beauty, strength, willfulness and wit attract every eligible man—and a few who shouldn't be so available. Mary has no interest in them, except to have a child. As the town tries to identify the father, we see what attracts them to this passionate Irish woman, particularly as she appears to the parish priest. He knows her attractions, does his best by her, and then suffers the consequences of his light hand and un-judging clerical spirit.

Recommended by: *The Washington Post Book World*

"...Keady's language falls like draped silk...all his characters possess immense delicacy of spirit."

Author Biography

Walter Keady grew up on a farm in the west of Ireland and worked in the Irish Civil Service. He served as a Catholic missionary priest in Brazil for several years. He is the author of *Celibates & Other Lovers*. Recently retired from IBM, he lives with his wife, Patricia, in New York's Hudson Valley.

Topics to Consider

1   Some have said this is an affectionate look at the Catholic church. Others have accused it of being highly critical. What do you think?

2   What is the basis for Mary choosing to remain silent about the father of her baby? Do you agree with that basis? Could there be another reason?

3   Define the nature of Mary's disobedience and discuss why it's so threatening to the townspeople. Do you think the reaction would be the same in the 1990s?

4   Does Mary ever truly pay a price for her decisions?

5   Is Mary a feminist? Is Rita?

6   What light does Kitty's apparent homosexuality cast on the moral questions in the novel?

7   Why does Kitty marry?

8   To what extent is Father Mulroe responsible for his own fate?

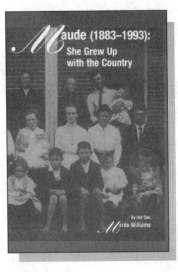

MAUDE (1883-1993)
She Grew Up with the Country

Author: Mardo Williams

Publisher: Calliope Press, 1996

Website: www.CalliopePress.com

Available in:
Hardcover, 335 pages. $22.95
(ISBN 0-9649241-2-9)

Genre: Nonfiction/Biography

Summary

During her 110-year lifetime, Maude Allen Williams went from oil lamps to a microwave oven, from the horse and buggy to an automobile. She stepped onto an airplane for the first time at age 77 to visit her daughter. Maude lived simply, suffered hardships, took in stride the time-consuming hand-labor of the 1900s—and, when she died at age 110, left family and friends with an enduring memory of her patience, kindness and courage, her quiet acceptance of the conditions over which she had no control, and the exemplary standards by which she lived. With great respect for detail in history, the book showcases the values and traditions of the pioneering families of American history.

Recommended by: Jim Cox, *Midwest Book Review*

*"**Maude** is an extraordinary and personal account of a memorable life and a kind of biographical window on the times and events through which she lived. Highly recommended."*

Author Biography

Mardo Williams, now age 93, began his writing career in 1927 as reporter for the daily Kenton *News-Republican*, eventually writing a daily business column for the Columbus *Dispatch*. Most recently, he has penned a children's book, patterned after the adventures of his four great-grandchildren. ***Great-Grandpa Fussy and the Little Puckerdoodles*** will be published Fall, 1999.

Topics to Consider

1 We are not given many details of Maude Allen's life before she married. How do you think her childhood might have prepared her for life as an adult? How was she prepared for the 36 years she lived as a widow?

2 Living for 110 years is an achievement in itself. Do you think the time span during which Maude lived was unique in its advancements and inventions or that any 100-year period would be equally characterized by change?

3 Was Maude's task of establishing herself as a wife and a mother much different from the challenge that faces a young woman today? In what ways was her job easier? In what ways harder?

4 Since the author is Maude's son, he is not likely to be an objective chronicler of her life. Does his attachment to her add to or detract from the story that he tells? How would you describe his writing style?

5 Do you feel that you know who Maude was as an individual? Did you connect with her emotionally? On any other levels?

6 Does this book make you long for the simplicity of "the good old days" or make you glad you live in the 1990s? In her life, did Maude embrace modernity or shun innovation?

7 Examine each of the following items and evaluate its meaning to Maude and its significance in her life: family, money, nature, humor, religion, community, fate.

8 On the back cover of the book, Maude is described as "an ordinary woman." Do you consider her to be ordinary?

9 Do you believe that Maude would think that our culture had advanced during her lifetime, separate from technological modernization?

10 What type of marriage did Lee Williams and Maude have?

"Divakaruni's prose is as lushly colorful as a closetful of saris, perfect for this airy, witty contemporary fairy tale."
—ENTERTAINMENT WEEKLY

·A NOVEL·

the Mistress of Spices

Chitra Banerjee Divakaruni
AUTHOR OF ARRANGED MARRIAGE

THE MISTRESS OF SPICES

Author: Chitra Banerjee Divakaruni

Publisher: Anchor Books, 1998

Website: www.randomhouse.com/ resources/bookgroup

Available in:
Paperback, 352 pages. $12.00
(ISBN 0-385-48238-8)

Genre: Fiction

Summary

Magic and reality collide in surprising ways in this national bestseller. Tilo is a young woman trained in the ancient art of spices and ordained as a mistress charged with special powers. Once fully initiated in a rite of fire, the now immortal Tilo—in the form of an old woman—travels through time to Oakland, California. There she opens a shop from which she administers healing spices to her customers. But an unexpected romance—forbidden to a mistress of spices—forces her to choose between immortality and love.

Recommended by: *The New Yorker*

"Divakaruni's prose is so pungent that it stains the page, yet beneath the sights and smells of this brand of magic realism she deftly introduces her true theme: how an ability to accommodate desire enlivens not only the individual heart but a society cornered by change."

Author Biography

Chitra Banerjee Divakaruni, born in India, is an award-winning poet who teaches creative writing at the University of Houston. She is also author of the short story collection *Arranged Marriage*, for which she she received three awards in 1995. Her fourth poetry collection, *Leaving Yuba City*, was published by Anchor in 1997, and her second novel, *Sister of My Heart*, will be available in hardcover from Doubleday in January, 1999.

Topics to Consider

1   Given a choice between a life of special powers and one of ordinary love and compassion, which would you choose? Were you satisfied with Tilo's choice?

2   Talk about the spices as a character in the novel.

3   Tilo only speaks her name out loud to one person in the novel. What is the role of names in the novel?

4   What do the spices take from Tilo? What do they give her? Is it a fair exchange?

5   Tilo speaks of "Anger whose other name is regret..." Discuss the dual nature of objects and feelings in the novel.

6   In what ways is punishment seen as a natural force? How is punishment and retribution tied to balance? Do you see retribution in a different light after reading this novel?

7   At one point in the novel, in regard to Geeta and her grandfather, Tilo says, "Better hate spoken than hate silent." Do you agree? Why or why not?

8   The author uses first person present tense in this novel, a choice not often used in fiction. What does this choice add to the novel?

9   What role does physical beauty play in this story? In Tilo's feelings about her body? About Raven? About the bougainvillea girls?

10 In return for Raven's story, Tilo tells him her name. A fair exchange?

11 Look closely at the structure of the novel. How does the author make use of the spices as chapter titles?

Editor's note: Additional topics for discussion may be found at www.randomhouse.com/resources/bookgroup

NIGHT RIDE HOME

Author: Barbara Esstman

Publisher: HarperPerennial, 1998

Website: www.harpercollins.com/
readers

Available in:
Paperback, 320 pages. $13.00
(ISBN 0-06-097754-X)

Genre: Fiction

Summary

In the days following World War II, Nora Mahler leads an ideal life, with her two children and the family horse ranch along the Missouri River. But her world suddenly comes apart when her son is killed in a riding accident. In his grief, Nora's husband dismantles the business and demands that she sell the ranch. When she refuses, he abandons her, taking their daughter with him to Chicago. Nora is devastated and Ozzie Kline, a horse wrangler who has longed for her since they were teenage lovers, comes to help rebuild the farm. Spending time together working the stables, Nora discovers a happiness she never found with her husband. But before they can realize their passion, her husband returns to the farm, determined to claim what he believes is his.

Recommended by: *St. Louis Post Dispatch*

*"What we're really celebrating in the romance of **Night Ride Home** is how to find yourself, not lose yourself."*

Author Biography

Barbara Esstman teaches writing and lives near Washington, D.C. **Night Ride Home** will be made into a Hallmark Hall of Fame movie for CBS in February of 1999.

Topics to Consider

1   Simon's death creates a "disorder" that goes beyond the tragedy inherent in the loss of a child. In many ways, Simon was the hub that connected the characters who narrate the novel. What did Simon mean to the other characters?

2   Contrast how Neal and Nora respond to Simon's death. Are there "right" and "wrong" ways to grieve? What are they?

3   When the tragedy occurs, Clea is a girl on the brink of becoming a woman. What has been modeled for her by the women in her life? Does she repeat or rebel against what she has seen?

4   What do you think was behind Neal's decision to subject Nora to shock therapy—a desire to help Nora or to subdue her independence? What responses to "undesirable behavior" occur today?

5   Ozzie was wounded in WW II and spent years wandering. How does the war appear to have affected Ozzie in ways of which even he is not aware?

6   Farm life is tied closely to the natural cycle of the seasons. The four sections of the novel correspond to the four seasons—spring through winter. What happens in each season? Do the events of each season reflect our common notions of spring, summer, fall and winter?

7   Late in the novel, Nora breaks down in Ozzie's truck after he has brought her to see an Arabian filly, Malaak. Why does Ozzie bring her back to talk to the filly's owner? What is he asking her to do? How is this the turning point of the novel for Nora?

8   Five characters take turns narrating the chapters of this book. Esstman has said that these are "all characters who have buried part of the truth." What do various characters see that others have "buried"? How would this novel be changed if it had a single narrator?

Editor's note: Additional topics for discussion may be found at www.harpercollins.com/readers

OUR MONEY OURSELVES
Redesigning Your
Relationship With Money

Author: Dr. C Diane Ealy
and Dr. Kay Lesh

Publisher: AMACOM, 1998

Website: www.amanet.org

Available in:
Paperback, 256 pages. $17.95
(ISBN 0-8144-7999-5)

Genre: Self Help/Personal Finance

Summary

No longer do women have to be the victims of negative, de-powering money messages such as *"It's unladylike to get involved with finances," "Someday my prince will come—and he'll provide for me,"* etc. With the help of this book, they can liberate themselves from disabling stereotypes and set a new standard for women relating to money—one where they're in control of their own financial fitness (not dependent on men), and where money is not something to worry over, feel guilty about, or be scared of, but rather something to enjoy and benefit from.

Recommended by: Patricia Eggers, VP, *Cablevision*

" This empowering guide will help women of all ages and occupations create a healthier and more profitable relationship with money —on their own terms."

Author Biography

C Diane Ealy, Ph.D. is one of the nation's leading specialists in women's creativity, a motivational presenter, and the author of *The Woman's Book of Creativity*. **Kay Lesh, Ph.D.** is a self-esteem specialist, a psychotherapist, and the co-author of *Building Self-Esteem*. They are frequent leaders of workshops on the topics of self-esteem, creativity, personal growth, and a variety of women's issues. Both authors live in Tucson, Arizona.

Topics to Consider

1   Men and women in relationships often argue about money. What are the triggers?

2   Little boys and girls often receive different messages about money. How does this affect their future relationships with money? What messages have young girls and women received? What did you "learn" about money when you were young?

3   The authors show how women can be victimized by negative money messages. If women are victims, who are the perpetrators? Did you think that there was any male-bashing in this book?

4   What are the most common ways in which bad relationships with money negatively affect women's lives?

5   What are some messages about money that the media currently give women?

6   Why do women, often even wealthy powerful women, feel guilty about spending money?

7   Discuss what the authors mean about money being a form of energy.

8   The authors talk about the spiritual nature of money—what do they mean? Many women struggle with this concept—why is that?

9   How do the money messages we get from our families affect us at work?

10 What should parents of teenage girls be telling their daughters about money?

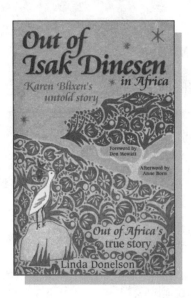

OUT OF ISAK DINESEN
Karen Blixen's untold story

Author: Linda Donelson

Publisher: Coulsong, 1998

Available in:
Paperback, 440 pages. $19.95
(ISBN 0-9643893-9-8)

Genre: Literature/Biography

Summary

Out of Isak Dinesen: Karen Blixen's untold story presents the first detailed account of Karen Blixen's life in Africa. Under the pseudonym Isak Dinesen, Baroness Blixen lyrically described her years on a pioneer coffee farm from 1914 to 1931. Some 70,000 travelers per year visit the Karen Blixen Museum near Nairobi. But those who want to know about the baroness's intriguing marriage to her cousin Bror and her great love affair with the legendary hunter Denys Finch Hatton will not find this information in her idealized memoir, *Out of Africa.* Using original letters, diaries, and excerpts from Isak Dinesen's stories, this award-winning biography portrays the young Karen Blixen in her struggle with a difficult marriage, a challenging coffee farm, and a complicated love affair in Africa.

Recommended by: *Kirkus Reviews*

"A book that traces the transformation of an unassuming young Danish bride into a regal if physically fragile grand dame of the veldt ...concrete and convincing."

Author Biography

Linda Donelson is a physician who once lived on a farm in Kenya overlooking Karen Blixen's land. Her book, *Out of Africa's true story*, has won two national awards—the Writer's Digest Grand Prize and the Paul Cowan Award for Nonfiction.

Topics to Consider

1 How does this portrait of Karen Blixen match your preconception of her?

2 How close to the real story was the Hollywood film **Out of Africa**?

3 What are the probable reasons Karen Blixen and Denys Finch Hatton never married?

4 What kind of person was the real Bror Blixen? How do you evaluate his role as husband?

5 What is your assessment of Karen Blixen's courage in going to Africa?

6 If you had lived Karen Blixen's life, at what juncture would you have selected a different choice of action?

7 In what ways can we today identify with Karen Blixen's struggles in exotic Africa? How do her problems have a timeless relevancy?

8 What was Karen Blixen's relationship with Africans?

9 Explain why you might have wanted, or may not have wanted, Karen Blixen to be your friend.

10 Explain how this biography of Isak Dinesen differs in its approach to the subject from others you've read.

OUTSIDE PASSAGE
A Memoir of an Alaskan Childhood

Author: Julia Scully

Publisher: Modern Library
(Random House), 1999

Website: www.randomhouse.com

Available in:
Paperback, 240 pages. $12.95
(ISBN 0-375-75240-4)

Genre: Nonfiction/Memoir

Summary

As this memoir opens, 11-year-old Julia Scully and her 13-year-old sister, Lillian, arrive alone in Nome, Alaska, circa 1940—a town notable for its barren extremes. Then, with the force of a jump cut, Scully rushes us further back in time and place. In San Francisco, four years earlier, she discovers her father's dead body in their dark apartment. "I don't know what happened next or even if I saw my father there on the kitchen floor. I just remember my sister and me running...back to the coffee shop, back to my mother, who didn't need to ask what we had found." Scully knows full well the heavy price she and her sister and mother, Rose, paid for familial silence as they searched for a livelihood and safe home in the frozen north.

Recommended by: Cleveland *Plain Dealer*

"Irresistible...It's a rare delight to find a book in which the setting and voice so perfectly mesh."

Author Biography

Julia Scully was born in Seattle, and moved with her mother and sister to Alaska before the outbreak of World War II. She went on to be editor-in-chief of *Modern Photography* for twenty years and was the co-discoverer of Mike Disfarmer's photographic portraits. She lives in Manhattan.

Topics to Consider

1   Dislocation often plays an important role in American literature and memoir. How does Julia Scully write about dislocation? What symbolizes her dislocation, both geographic and emotional?

2   Alaska in the 1930s was both bleak and beautiful—two words that also describe Scully's childhood. How does the Alaskan landscape reflect the torment and tenderness of young Julia's life?

3   Why do you think the author wrote **Outside Passage** in the present tense? How does this affect the reading of the book? What would have been different if Scully had used the past tense?

4   Julia recounts her mother's advice that "You have to guard against disappointment, against hurt and, above all, against sadness." (Page 146.) How does her mother live her own advice? How is it reflected in each of her two daughters?

5   Julia is affected by the scene with Chief Yaeger and the malemute. Her mother tells her, "You can't cry for everything in this world" (page 151), yet Julia keeps on crying and says, "I can't stop. I don't want to stop." Julia's mother comments that the dog "was just a stray." How is Julia different from her mother? From her sister, Lillian?

6   Abandonment is a theme throughout the memoir. Discuss how abandonment surfaces in relationships, jobs, and sense of place.

7   Why do you think Julia steals the curtains?

8   "Hands-off" is the phrase Julia uses to describe her mother's approach to parenting. How would you describe Rose as a mother? How did she balance her needs with those of her daughters?

9   Julia wonders whether she's "weak" because she feels emotions (page 166). What is your view of the young woman Julia has become—is she weak? Does she have any role model for achieving her goals? What are the personal challenges she may face in college? What strengths in her character will help her in college and later in life?

THE PILOT'S WIFE

Author: Anita Shreve

Publisher: Little, Brown & Co., 1998

Website: www.littlebrown.com

Available in:
Hardcover, 293 pages. $23.95
(ISBN 0-316-78908-9)

Genre: Fiction

Summary

Being married to a pilot has taught Kathryn Lyons to be ready for emergencies, but nothing has prepared her for the late-night knock on her door and the news of her husband's fatal crash. As Kathryn struggles through her grief, she is forced to confront disturbing rumors about the man she loved and the life that she took for granted. Torn between her impulse to protect her husband's memory and her desire to know the truth, Kathryn sets off to find out if she ever really knew the man who was her husband. In her determination to test the truth of her marriage, she faces shocking revelations about the secrets a man can keep and the actions a woman is willing to take.

Recommended by: *Newsday*

"From cover to rapidly reached cover, **The Pilot's Wife** *is beautifully plotted, tensely paced, and thoroughly absorbing."*

Author Biography

Anita Shreve is the author of the acclaimed novels *The Weight of Water, Resistance, Eden Close, Strange Fits of Passion,* and *Where or When.* Her award-winning short stories and nonfiction have appeared in the *New York Times Magazine, Cosmopolitan,* and *Esquire.* She lives in western Massachusetts.

Topics to Consider

1   The complex relationship between secrecy and intimacy is an important theme of *The Pilot's Wife*. Consider the secrets kept by the following characters: Kathryn, Jack, Mattie, Robert, Muire. In each case, what motivates the deceiver? Who is protected and who is harmed by the secret? When, if ever, can deception be an expression of love?

2   Examine the conversation between Kathryn and Mattie (pp. 114-115), especially Mattie's question: "But how do you ever know that you know a person?" Is there a more satisfactory answer to this question than the one Kathryn offers?

3   Muire revealed the whole truth to Kathryn about Jack's secret life. How did this confession help Kathryn find the answers to her questions about how "real" her marriage was? Who is the "real wife?" (p. 265)

4   As a mother, is Kathryn obligated, at some future time, to share full knowledge of Jack with Mattie? Which parent do you think shared the stronger relationship with Mattie?

5   In what way was the house that Kathryn and Jack lived in for 11 years a metaphor for their relationship? Discuss the significance of Kathryn's discovery of the site of the Sisters' Chapel at the end of the book.

6   What devices does Shreve use to make her novel such a compelling read? Consider the flashbacks, the action, the style of language and word choice, and character painting.

PRAYING FOR BASE HITS
An American Boyhood

Author: Bruce Clayton

Publisher: University of
Missouri Press, 1998

Website:
www.system.missouri.edu/upress

Available in:
Paperback, 276 pages. $16.95
(ISBN 0-8262-1189-5)

Genre: Memoir

Summary

More than a chronicle of his growing-up years in Kansas City, **Bruce Clayton**'s narrative taps the commonalities of the fifties and conveys the innocence, simplicity, and naiveté of the era. Shifting from impish boyhood escapades to persistent family tensions and back again, *Praying for Base Hits* elicits a wide range of emotions. The final chapters of the memoir find Clayton trading his dashed childhood hopes of becoming a New York Yankee for the mysteries of the adult world. Skillfully alternating between the voices of youth and adulthood, Clayton reflects on his boyhood fully aware that he can never return.

Recommended by: John Egerton

"A charming, evocative, nostalgic paean to a midcentury way of life that has largely vanished ... even those who got here too late for the '50s can share in the vicarious pleasures of that deceptively simple time."

Author Biography

Bruce Clayton is Harry A. Logan Sr. Professor of History at Allegheny College in Meadville, PA. He is the author or editor of several books, including *Forgotten Prophet: The Life of Randolph Bourne* and *W.J. Cash: A Life.*

Topics to Consider

1 Is there a generation for whom this book is more accessible? If so, which one and why? Is *Praying for Base Hits* meaningful to both men and women?

2 Was Clayton's relationship with his "Old Man" typical of the time period? How do parental relationships differ today?

3 As a neighbor and confidant, Mr. Jim played a significant role in Clayton's childhood. Is it common for youngsters to have such friends today? If not, what accounts for the difference? More alternatives for entertainment? Fear and mistrust?

4 Compare the deep love of baseball that Clayton and his pals felt to the recent interest in a new record being set for home runs. Do young boys today still feel the same way about baseball?

5 Religion was a major factor in Clayton's childhood. How did this affect the rest of his life? How does his experience compare to your own?

6 Over the course of the memoir, Clayton realizes that Old Man Pierce is not simply a mean-spirited old man but a blatant racist. What particular incidents revealed Mr. Pierce's true nature? Can you remember any signs of racism from your own childhood that you may have overlooked or misunderstood at the time?

7 Clayton looks back upon the lives of his grandfather and father and realizes the few options they truly had as working class men. How did Clayton's father help him escape a similar fate?

8 Were the children of the 1950s more innocent than children are today? If so, why?

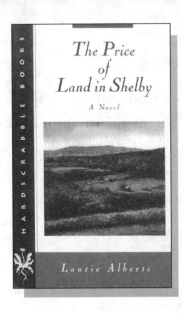

THE PRICE OF LAND IN SHELBY

Author: Laurie Alberts

Publisher: University Press of New England, 1997

Website: www.dartmouth.edu/acad-inst/upne/

Available in:
Paperback, 330 pages. $14.95
(ISBN 0-87451-844-X)

Genre: Fiction

Summary

Shelby, Vermont, is a place torn between stasis and change, a contemporary New England town "where time was revealed not by geology, but by tumbling stone walls" and, increasingly, the division of family farms into "executive lots" where rich Flatlanders build expensive homes. Against this backdrop the 30-year saga of the Chartrain family is played out in a novel both searing in its portrayal of the realities behind the picture postcard views and incisive in its truths about the indomitability of the human spirit.

Recommended by: *Booklist*

"Wedding a highly polished technique to gritty, keenly observed details, Alberts has written a wonderful story about a family full of crazy hope."

Author Biography

Laurie Alberts is author of *Goodnight Silky Sullivan* (1995) and the Michener Award-winning *Tempting Fate* (1987). She lives in southeastern Vermont and teaches at Hampshire College. Her new novel, *Lost Daughters*, will be published by University Press of New England in March, 1999.

Topics to Consider

1   Though the Chartrain family suffers a number of tragedies, the survivors manage to retain a persistent belief that they can remake and improve their lives. What is the source of this hope and how do each of the Chartrain siblings manifest it?

2   What makes Mitchell Chartrain, a dreamer, frequent failure, and occasional petty criminal, a sympathetic character? How does Mitchell's need for his father's approval shape his life? How does he break free from this crippling desire?

3   In the early chapters, Donna Chartrain is a bold, adventurous teenager. Which aspects of her teenage personality resonate with (and perhaps create) her later troubles? How much of young Donna is retained by the end of the book, how much is lost?

4   The family land is both a source of strength and conflict for this family. What does the land mean to Jamie? Mitchell? The sisters? Lowell? Gramp? How do Jamie's attempts to hold the land together and Mitchell's attempts to escape it function both in terms of their own lives and their relationship to one another?

5   In what way do the Chartrains find identity and strength in family? In what way are they harmed by it?

6   Lowell gets only one brief chapter from his own point of view. Why do you think the author decided to include Lowell's perspective, and how does it add to your understanding of the dynamics of the Chartrain clan?

7   What social and economic forces have contributed to the poverty of the Chartrain family? Why are they "downwardly mobile" in comparison to their grandparents? What psychological and economic influences do the newly arrived "flatlanders" have on the Chartrains and their neighbors?

8   The author has said that she intended each chapter to be able stand alone as a separate short story. Which of the chapters do you think function as stories? What makes this book a novel and not just a collection of connected stories? What about this storytelling approach is suited to the subject matter of *The Price of Land in Shelby*?

THE READER

Author: Bernhard Schlink

Publisher: Vintage Books
(Random House), 1998

Website: www.randomhouse.com/
vintage/read

Available in:
Paperback, 224 pages. $11.00
(ISBN 0-679-78130-7)

Genre: Fiction

Summary

Postwar Germany is the setting for this novel. Michael Berg is fifteen and suffering from hepatitis. When he gets sick in the street one day on his way home from school, a woman brings him into her apartment and helps him to wash up. Later, he visits the woman to thank her and is drawn into a love affair that is as intoxicating as it is unusual—their meetings become a ritual of reading aloud, taking showers, and making love. When Hanna disappears following a misunderstanding, Michael is overcome with guilt and loss. When Michael next sees her, he is a young law student and Hanna is on trial for a hideous crime. But as he watches her refuse to defend herself, Michael gradually realizes that his former lover may be guarding a secret she considers more shameful than murder.

Recommended by: *The New York Times Book Review*

"Moving, suggestive and ultimately hopeful...[The Reader] leaps national boundaries and speaks straight to the heart."

Author Biography

Bernhard Schlink was born in Germany in 1944. A professor of law at the University of Berlin and a practicing judge, he is also the author of several prize-winning crime novels. He lives in Bonn and Berlin.

Topics to Consider

1 Discuss the difference in social class between Hanna and Michael, and how it becomes manifest throughout the novel.

2 Why is the sense of smell so important in this story? What is it about Hanna that so strongly provokes the boy's desire?

3 In a novel so suffused with guilt, how is Michael guilty? Does his narrative serve as a way of putting himself on trial? What verdict does he reach? Is he asking readers to examine the evidence he presents and to condemn him or exonerate him? Or has he already condemned himself?

4 Is Michael's father deserving of his son's scorn and disappointment? Is Michael's love for Hanna meant, in part, to be an allegory for his generation's implication in their parents' guilt?

5 Why does Michael visit the concentration camp at Struthof? What is he seeking? What does he find instead?

6 What do you think of Michael's decision to send Hanna the tapes?

7 One might argue that Hanna didn't willfully collaborate with Hitler's genocide and that her decisions were driven only by a desire to hide her secret. Does this view exonerate Hanna in any way? Are there any mitigating circumstances in her case?

8 Why does Hanna do what she does at the end of the novel?

9 How does this novel leave you feeling and thinking? Is it hopeful or ultimately despairing? If you have read other Holocaust literature, how does *The Reader* compare?

Editor's note: Additional topics for discussion may be found at www.randomhouse.com/vintage/read

RETURN TO THE SEA
Reflections on
Anne Morrow Lindbergh's
Gift From The Sea

Author: Anne M. Johnson

Publisher: Innisfree Press, 1998

Available in:
Paperback, 144 pages. $11.95
(ISBN 1-880913-24-0)

Genre: Nonfiction/
Spirituality/Women's Studies

Summary

In 1955, Anne Morrow Lindbergh struck a spiritual chord with women in her classic bestseller *Gift from the Sea*. Her message then—of simplicity and solitude, of quieting and centering—is needed more than ever as women today struggle to balance career and family with their creative, spiritual needs. In *Return to the Sea*, Anne Johnson leads women back to Lindbergh's "beach" and lets the shells be our teachers once again. Using her own experiences as a mother, career woman, and therapist, Johnson offers a renewed vision of intentional space for personal and spiritual growth through reflection and journaling. Like a well-worn copy of Lindbergh's classic hiding deep in your bookshelf, 'the sea of inner stillness' awaits patiently for your inevitable return.

Recommended by: Reeve Lindbergh

*"I know **Gift from the Sea** almost by heart because it is written in my mother's voice. But I think I will come to know [this book] almost as well. The two [books] resonate beautifully."*

Author Biography

Anne M. Johnson, MSW, is a licensed clinical social worker. She has worked in a variety of settings as a psychotherapist and as an educator on topics related to parenting, family dynamics, and spirituality. She is co-author of *The Essence of Parenting* (1995). Anne lives with her family in Lake Mills, Wisconsin.

Topics to Consider

1   If you've read *Gift from the Sea* when you were younger, what impact did it have on you then? If you've reread it recently (or read it for the first time), what is your response now?

2   The author describes a favorite vacation spot where she felt content. Is there a place you have visited where you have felt this kind of contentment? What qualities of this place inspires these feelings?

3   What are the top three things that you think every child deserves? In what ways do you give yourself these things? How do they affect your mental health and attitude? What are you missing?

4   What has preoccupied your thoughts this week? How might "mental housecleaning" change your energy level, free up your time, nourish your soul?

5   What does the phrase "the art of shedding" (page 54) suggest to you? What are the signals in your life that it is time to start shedding? What might you most like to shed at this point?

6   How would you describe your five-year-old self? Yourself at fifteen? As an adult? What part of "you" is present in all?

7   Does the thought of spending time alone entice you? Ideally, where would you like to go? What would you do? How might you introduce this kind of experience into your everyday life?

8   What is your idea of "perfection"? In what way has your "imperfection" defined you? Confined you? Helped you?

9   What are the "shells" that surround you? How do they protect you? Are there any you have outgrown?

10 How might your life be different if you spent quality time alone? For an extended time each year? How might others benefit from your absence? From your renewed return?

11 What philosophy do you espouse that helps you make sense of the ups and downs of life? Is there a guiding principle that gives meaning to the past and keeps you hopeful and optimistic about the future?

ROSALIND
A FAMILY ROMANCE

Author: Myra Goldberg

Publisher: Zoland Books, 1998

Website: www.zolandbooks.com

Available in:
Paperback, 241 pages. $13.00
(ISBN 0-944072-60-7)

Genre: Fiction

Summary

Rosalind Oliner, a family therapist with a strong intellect and a controlling emotional style, runs her immediate and extended family. "She'd been lucky in work, lucky in love...only her body eluded her." At thirty-seven she has open heart surgery and, unable to face her fear of death, retreats into self-destructiveness, leaving the people around her to take charge of everything previously left to her. Power shifts, as the members of the family dance reconfigure themselves to fill the void. Sisters, husbands, children who all spun about Rosalind like satellites now take their places in the new cosmology, and Rosalind learns that mortality is just another fact of being human. This novel is about the '80s, family life, middle-aged baby boomers, mixed marriages, and mother and daughters, as well as the pain of mortality. (With a little help from *Middlemarch* and *As You Like It*.)

Recommended by: Grace Paley

"I love the stuff. Deeply serious and very funny."

Author Biography

Myra Goldberg teaches in the graduate writing program at Sarah Lawrence College. Her first book, ***Whistling and Other Stories*** (Zoland, 1993) was a *New York Times* Notable Book of the Year. She lives in New York City with her daughter.

Topics to Consider

1   How does Rosalind wield power over other members of her family?

2   Is her way of dealing with other people any different from the way she deals with herself? What is she scared of?

3   If Ros is secret, quixotic, and full of rationalizations, she is also empathic, and interested in other people, life and learning. Does a character whose flaws and virtues are inextricably linked strike you as realistic? What are the intertwined strengths and weaknesses of Henry, Lila, and Lev?

4   How and why do Henry, Lila, and Lev turn this family around? Do their difficulties taking action have anything to do with Ros?

5   What is Ros's place in the family at the end of the book?

6   How are people's choices in this novel affected by the times they are living in?

7   What is the novel saying about Yuppie (or middle class) culture, and death?

8   What is the bear doing here?

9   How does the notion of strangeness vs. familiarity play itself out in the various marriages and alliances in the book?

SARAH CONLEY

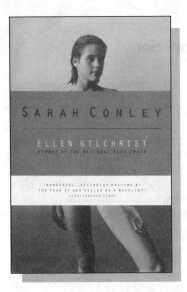

Author: Ellen Gilchrist

Publisher: Back Bay Books (Little, Brown & Co.), 1997

Website: www.littlebrown.com

Available in:
Paperback, 264 pages. $13.00
(ISBN 0-316-31492-7)

Genre: Fiction

Summary

When Sarah Conley, a celebrated magazine editor and writer in New York City, returns home to the South to visit an ailing childhood friend, she finds herself forced to choose between pursuing her career and rekindling her relationship with the man she has long considered the love of her life. In a novel widely praised for its energy, passion, and wit, Ellen Gilchrist brings into brilliant focus the quandaries that arise when we realize our heart's desire.

Recommended by: Miranda Schwartz, *Chicago Tribune*

"Touching and intelligent ... the love affair of Sarah Conley is hopeful and precarious—like life itself."

Author Biography

Ellen Gilchrist is the critically acclaimed author of fourteen previous books, including the National Book Award-winning *Victory Over Japan*. A new collection of stories, *Flights of Angels*, has just been published. She lives in Fayetteville, Arkansas.

Topics to Consider

1   Sarah Conley faces the quintessential writer's dilemma—whether to use the events of her life as material in her fiction. Do you agree with her decision on this matter? How do life and art interact for Sarah?

2   Was it Sarah's book that led the friendship between Sarah and Eugenie into a dormant state? What else could have led the two to drift apart?

3   When Sarah receives the call that Eugenie is dying, her thought is "My past lies dying and I must go to her." In what ways was Sarah's past dying?

4   What was Eugenie's motive in inviting Sarah to visit her on her death bed? What role do you believe Eugenie had in the timing of her own death?

5   Would Sarah's relationship with Jack have continued had Elise lived? What role does Elise play in Sarah's reflection of her past?

6   How does the house in the country symbolize elements of Sarah's life?

7   Throughout her life, Sarah learns to take care of herself. Were her mechanisms for doing this more helpful or hurtful?

8   Robert claims Sarah was lucky. Was she? Did Sarah feel lucky?

9   Truth is Sarah's religion. (p. 48) Discuss Sarah's choices in telling the truth about her own life. When is the truth revealed and when is it not?

10 Discuss Jack's readiness for another marriage.

11 How does Sarah's perception of the role of work in her life change throughout the book? What circumstances lead her to re-evaluate the importance of her work and the scope of her career?

12 If you could write another chapter to this book, how would you unfold the story? What are the challenges to Jack and Sarah's relationship? What are their opportunities?

SNAKE

Author: Kate Jennings
Publisher: Little, Brown & Co., 1998
Website: www.littlebrown.com
Available in:
Paperback, 176 pages. $12.00
(ISBN 0-316-91258-1)
Genre: Fiction

Summary

Set against the hard landscape of postwar Australia and moving through the 1950s and 1960s, *Snake* starts with a premise as frightening and commonplace as the deadly bush snake that lurks in the Australian interior: The loyal Rex, a good man, cherishes his wife Irene. Irene, bubbling over with feminine anger and unspecified desire, despises Rex. Into this marriage, this terrible emptiness, two people pour their very lives. *Snake* is about the loneliness of men married to unkind women, about the unloved becoming unlovable.

Recommended by: Jill Ker Conway

"As spare and compelling as the landscape of her native country. The reader can feel the heat and smell the disillusionment of this Australian rural scene, captured in breathtaking detail."

Author Biography

Kate Jennings is the author of *Cats, Dogs, and Pitchforks* (poetry), *Bad Manners* (essays), and the prize-winning fiction collection *Women Falling Down in the Street*, among other books. A leading figure in the Australian feminist movement, she has made her home in New York City since 1979.

Topics to Consider

1   How do Rex and Irene find one another and marry? How does disappointment come to define their marriage? Are either of them in control of their lives? Do either of them have a sense of personal power?

2   When Irene shakes her head in judgment of Girlie's fear of snakes and says, "Poor Girlie, such a scaredy-cat!", is she being cruel or is she commenting on some larger rule of life that Girlie had better realize if she is to survive? What do you think the different images of snakes in the novel come to represent?

3   Irene lines up Girlie and Boy to teach them about the botany of irises and tells them that "unlike people, flowers never disappoint." What does she mean by this? Why does Irene garden?

4   Irene finds Girlie irritating and adores Boy. Explore her tempestuous relationship with her children. What sort of a mother do you find her to be? Do you feel sympathetic to her frustrations at being a mother?

5   Rex seems like a visitor in his own home. He is "permanently distracted" and no help to either of his children. What are the defining moments of his relationship with Girlie and Boy? What sort of a father is he?

6   How does religion figure into the lives of Rex and Irene? Without a religion do they have any kind of spirituality?

7   At the end of the novel, after Irene leaves Rex, he obsessively walks the land, then buys pigs and gives them the run of the farm, especially Irene's garden. Why does he do this? What do you think is happening to him? Does his suicide reveal anything more about him than we already know?

8   Irene walks out on Rex without a word and leaves with another man for the north. How does she change her own life by leaving Rex?

9   How does the Australian landscape play a part in the lives of these people? Does it become a metaphor for the spiritual desolation in which they find themselves?

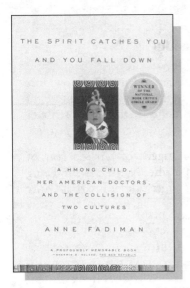

THE SPIRIT CATCHES YOU AND YOU FALL DOWN
A Hmong child, her American doctors, and the collision of two cultures

Author: Anne Fadiman

Publisher: Farrar, Straus & Giroux, 1998

Website: www.fsgee.com

Available in:
Paperback, 358 pages. $13.00
(ISBN 0-374-52564-1)

Genre: Nonfiction/Cultural Studies

Summary

The Spirit Catches You and You Fall Down explores the clash between a small county hospital in California and a refugee family from Laos over the care of Lia Lee, a Hmong child diagnosed with severe epilepsy. Lia's parents and her doctors both wanted what was best for Lia, but the lack of understanding between them led to tragedy. Winner of the National Book Critics Circle Award for Nonfiction, the *Los Angeles Times* Book Prize for Current Interest, and the *Boston Book Review* Rea Award for Nonfiction, Anne Fadiman's compassionate account of this cultural impasse is literary journalism at its finest.

Recommended by: Linnea Lannon, *The Detroit Free Press*

"...Explores issues of culture, immigration, medicine, and the war in [Laos] with such skill that it's nearly impossible to put down."

Author Biography

Anne Fadiman is the editor of *The American Scholar.* Recipient of a National Magazine Award for Reporting, she has written for *Civilization, Harper's, Life,* and *The New York Times,* among other publications. She lives in New York City.

Topics to Consider

1 What do you think of traditional Hmong birth practices? Compare them to the techniques used when Lia was born. How do Hmong and American birth practices differ?

2 The author says, "I was struck...by the staggering toll of stress that the Hmong exacted from the people who took care of them." Why do you think the doctors felt such great stress?

3 Dr. Neil Ernst felt that it was unacceptable behavior for the Hmong to deviate from certain rules dictated by our knowledge of medicine. Do you think the Hmong understood this message? Why or why not? What do you think of Neil and Peggy?

4 Of the doctors who were able to communicate with the Hmong, how were they able to do so? What might be learned from this?

5 How did you feel about the Lees' refusal to give Lia her medicine? Can you understand their motivation? Do you sympathize with it?

6 How did you feel about Child Protective Services taking Lia away from her parents? Was foster care ultimately to Lia's benefit or detriment?

7 How does the greatest of all Hmong folktales, the story of how Shee Yee fought with nine evil *dab* brothers (p. 170), reflect the life and culture of the Hmong?

8 What are the most important aspects of Hmong culture? What do the Hmong consider their most important duties and obligations? How did they affect the Hmong's transition to life in the United States?

9 Despite the heroic efforts of Lia's doctors, and that her parents cared for her deeply, this arguably preventable tragedy still occurred. Can you think of anything that might have prevented it?

10 Would you assign blame for Lia's tragedy? If so, to whom? What do you think the author feels about this question?

SPLIT
A Counterculture Childhood

Author: Lisa Michaels

Publisher: Mariner Books, 1999

Website: www.hmco.com

Available in:
Paperback, 288 pages. $13.00
(ISBN 0-395-95788-5)

Genre: Nonfiction/Memoir

Summary

In *Split*, Lisa Michaels offers a strikingly textured portrait of her days of communes and road trips, of antiwar protests and rallies—and of what came after, for her parents and for herself—as the radicalism of the 1960s and '70s gave way to conservative times. As a young child, Lisa visited her father in prison, where he was serving a two-year sentence for his part in an antiwar protest. In the early '70s, she toured the country with her mother and stepfather in a customized mail truck. By the age of eight Lisa was a veteran leaflet-folder, and she consecrated her father's second marriage in a Berkeley park by reading from *Quotations from Chairman Mao*. Not surprisingly, Lisa grew up craving conformity, but she also came to share many of the values her parents held dear: independence, frankness, and unsparing self-examination.

Recommended by: Susan Cheever, *L.A. Times Book Review*

"The intersection of intimate, personal, day-to-day lives with the cataclysmic events of recent history gives this book tremendous power."

Author Biography

Lisa Michaels is a contributing editor at *Threepenny Review*. A recipient of the San Francisco Foundation award in nonfiction, she has written for *Glamour, Salon,* and the *New York Times Magazine.* She lives with her husband in Seattle.

Topics to Consider

1 Lisa Michaels gives her memoir, *Split*, the subtitle "a counter-culture childhood." Was her childhood more a product of her parents' divorce or of the cultural context of her parents' lives?

2 What is Lisa's opinion of the causes her parents supported?

3 Do you believe Lisa's parents behaved responsibly toward her? If you were her parent, would you have acted differently?

4 When do sacrifices have to be made in this family? By whom?

5 Sometimes Lisa muses on the accuracy of her memories. What do you think determines which memories we retain from childhood? Which matters most: what actually happened or what you remember?

6 What values was Lisa taught? How did she demonstrate them when she became an adult?

7 As both of her parents remarry, are there any parallels between their situations and the adjustments Lisa must make as she moves between her two families?

8 What would you identify as the crisis points in Lisa's life? Are there other ways she could have handled them?

9 At one point Lisa describes herself as "full of outsize moods, outsize expectations for feedback and affection, someone to ground me." (p. 244) Why did she feel this way? How did her behavior exhibit these needs?

10 Does Lisa Michaels have a special story to tell? If so, in what way?

THE STORM

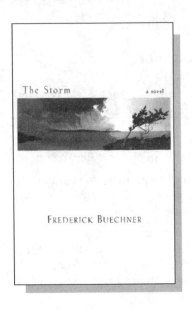

Author: Frederick Buechner

Publisher:
HarperSanFrancisco, 1998

Website: www.harpercollins.com

Available in:
Hardcover, 208 pages. $18.00
(ISBN 0-06-061144-8)

Genre: Fiction

Summary

Set on wealthy Plantation Island in South Florida, *The Storm* is the story of a family and the interconnections that tie their past to the present. It is the story of two estranged brothers embarking on journeys of self-discovery and reconciliation. Kenzie Maxwell is a patrician writer who enjoys life with his rich third wife but muses daily on the sins of his past. Two decades ago, Kenzie was forced to leave New York because of a scandal, and has never forgiven his brother for the part he played. Now it's the eve of Kenzie's 70th birthday, and a storm is brewing. Kenzie must somehow contrive to reconcile with his brother—and make peace with his past.

Recommended by: *Kirkus Reviews*

*"A wonderfully humane and satisfying meditative romance ...
A marvelous adaptation of Shakespeare—one of the best ever."*

Author Biography

Frederick Buechner is the author of thirty works of fiction and nonfiction, including, most recently, the novel *On the Road with the Archangel.* His novel *Godric* was nominated for the Pulitzer Prize and *The Book of Bebb* was nominated for a National Book Award. His nonfiction books include *Wishful Thinking: A Theological ABC* and *Listening to Your Life.* He lives in Vermont.

Topics to Consider

1   Kenzie sometimes felt that the richest gift he could give Kia was to let her alone, and that it might be best for him too. Yet the depth of his feeling for her lasted a lifetime. How do you reconcile inner voices of passion and reason when they clearly conflict?

2   Do you agree or disagree with Dalton's "afterthought" to share Kenzie's personal letter with the media (page 25)? Are there circumstances where family loyalty, i.e. the desire to protect a loved one, is more important than having someone suffer the consequences of their actions?

3   Dalton never could understand why Kenzie would never want to see him again, just as Kenzie can't understand why Dalton would vilify Kia. Do you side more with Dalton or with Kenzie? Why? What does *The Storm* have to say about "forgiveness?"

4   Kenzie wants to know if, "even in Heaven, do they say 'If only...?'" What would you tell him?

5   Kenzie often wondered whether he was as mad as Dalton (page 79). What do you think? Was he?

6   Kenzie reflects on what it feels like to be seventy (page 160), and how he believes "the end will come as a friend." As a result, were you forced to examine your own attitudes about aging and dying? Was it uncomfortable to do so?

7   The desire to know and see God causes some to turn to religion, others to meditation, still others to insanity. What does *The Storm* suggest about the presence of a higher power in our lives?

8   Do you think the title of this book refers more to the storm described in Chapter 11, or to the tumultuousness of the characters' innermost thoughts and feelings?

9   In more than one place, *The Storm* echoes William Shakespeare's *The Tempest*. If you were to read (or re-read) *The Tempest*, do you think that similar discussion topics would apply?

SURRENDERING TO MOTHERHOOD
Losing Your Mind, Finding Your Soul

Author: Iris Krasnow

Publisher: Hyperion, 1997

Available in:
Paperback, 212 pages. $12.95
(ISBN 0-7868-8318-9)

Genre: Nonfiction/
Women's Studies/Parenting

Summary

Iris Krasnow was a woman who seemed to have it all, including a glamorous job as a feature writer for UPI, which took her around the country and the world. Yet no matter what she achieved in her journalistic ascent, a relentless angst gnawed at her heart; she felt a spiritual void. Ultimately—and ironically—it took the chaotic joy of motherhood for Krasnow to find peace. By age thirty-nine, she and her husband were the parents of four young sons. Her children had captured her, forcing her to live in the now, and she was surrendering. This memoir is about letting go of the burning need to achieve, and finding your true self in the love and calamity of motherhood.

Recommended by: Dr. Steven R. Covey

"These pages follow the author's remarkable journey into motherhood as she travels from doubt and confusion into understanding and acceptance and finds that what is most personal is most general. A profound, moving odyssey!"

Author Biography

Iris Krasnow is a freelance writer whose work regularly appears in *The Washington Post.* Her articles have also been featured in *Life, Self,* and *The Wall Street Journal.* She lives in Maryland with her husband and four sons.

Topics to Consider

1 How does Krasnow's image of her mother change after she becomes a mother herself?

2 One of the important influences on Krasnow's way of thinking was Zelda Fichandler, who said that she doesn't believe her career kept her from being there when her children needed her, "but I don't think I was always there when I needed them." Krasnow notes that the children of her career-oriented friends don't appear to be suffering, but their mothers do—pulled in all directions. Would you agree with these assessments?

3 Will women of succeeding generations experience transformations similar to Krasnow's or are her experiences unique to women who came to adulthood in the '60s and '70s?

4 Though Krasnow calls him an equal partner, her husband Chuck makes only occasional appearances in the last two sections of the book. Do you think Chuck's journey as a father came with the same dramatic, emotional transformations as Krasnow experienced?

5 Some may argue that Krasnow enjoys a number of advantages that many other mothers do not—she is already very successful, easily finds work that suits her desired schedule, and can afford domestic help. Do these factors make it harder for women without such advantages to relate to the advice she offers?

6 How does Krasnow's view of feminism change over the years?

7 Do you believe that Krasnow could have found a similar level of spiritual fulfillment if she had never had children?

8 How do you see the roles of mothers and fathers evolving in the coming decades?

9 Has this book changed the way you think about your role as a parent or spouse?

TALKING TO THE DEAD

Author: Helen Dunmore

Publisher: Back Bay Books
(Little, Brown & Co.), 1996

Website: www.littlebrown.com

Available in:
Paperback, 300 pages. $12.95
(ISBN 0-316-19645-2)

Genre: Fiction

Summary

Nina and Isabel are the closest of sisters, bound together by the devastating memory of the baby brother who died in his crib twenty-five years before. But when Isabel gives birth to her first child, and Nina journeys to the country to help look after her, images from the past rush back. Each sister claims to possess knowledge that could destroy the other. Who is lying, and who is telling the truth? Against the backdrop of the hottest summer in a century, a drama of suspicion and betrayal unfolds.

Recommended by: Carol Kino, *New York Times Book Review*

"Gripping and complex ... a moral whodunit."

Author Biography

Helen Dunmore, winner of Britain's first-ever Orange Prize for the year's best novel by a woman, is a writer of novels, short stories, and poetry. She lives in Bristol, England, with her husband and children.

Topics to Consider

1   Nina describes the way that she and Isabel marveled at their personality differences in their childhood. Growing up, each sister played upon her unique qualities as "a game that eventually played us." What did Nina mean by this? How were the sisters "played" by this game?

2   Richard and Edward figure prominently in that they extract unique information about Nina and Isabel. What do these men bring out of each of the sisters?

3   What does Nina's affinity for food and sex symbolize? Contrast with Isabel's anorexia and frigidity.

4   What role does the climate, especially the heat, play in the story?

5   Our understanding of story is often molded by the point of view from which it is told. Discuss how you think the portrayal of the characters, and the depiction of specific scenes throughout the story would vary if told from Isabel's perspective.

6   How and why did your perceptions of what happened to Colin change throughout the novel?

7   Is there a justification for Nina's affair with Richard? What does she have that Isabel does not?

8   What is the significance of the final scene?

TEMPEST RISING

Author: Diane McKinney-Whetstone

Publisher: Quill (Wm. Morrow), 1999

Website: www.williammorrow.com

Available in:
Paperback, 280 pages. $12.00
(ISBN 0-688-16640-7)

Genre: Fiction

Summary

Clarise, Finch, and their three adolescent daughters are living the dream life of the black financially privileged when suddenly Finch's lucrative catering business falls on hard times and Clarise suffers an apparent nervous collapse. The daughters are discharged into the foster care of Mae, a politically connected card shark, and her stunningly beautiful, yet mean-spirited, daughter, Ramona. The girls' presence in and subsequent disappearance from Mae's house force Mae and Ramona to confront the brutal secret that caused their hearts to lock against one another.

Recommended by: *Publishers Weekly*

"[A] remarkable first novel...The story probes beneath its residents' lives to tell a powerful tale of damage and healing."

Author Biography

Diane McKinney-Whetstone is the author of the national bestseller *Tumbling*. She is a regular contributor to *Philadelphia Magazine* and her work has appeared in *Essence* and the Sunday *Philadelphia Inquirer Magazine*. She is the recipient of numerous awards, including a Pennsylvania Council on the Arts grant. She teaches fiction writing at her alma mater, the University of Pennsylvania, and lives with her husband, Greg, and teenage twins outside Philadelphia. Note: the author is available for reading group conference calls; call 212/261-6570 for details.

Topics to Consider

1 When the author was growing up in the 1950s and '60s, there were few prominent black writers, especially female ones. Now, a whole new genre of books by African American women writers is gaining ground. How do you think the author's early reading experiences shaped her as a writer? Do her books speak only to black audiences, or do they have universal, cross-over appeal?

2 Recount the number and variety of ways in which the author uses food to convey a mood, describe a character, or mark a change in the plot. Are all these food references positive in nature? Can you recall other novels whose plots and characters hinged on references to food and eating?

3 In *Tempest Rising*, the definition of "family" is altered by the author's use of aunts and uncles, rather than traditional parents, in raising Clarise. Did this pose advantages and/or disadvantages to the nurturing she received? Did Clarise's relationship with her aunts and uncles have bearing upon her own daughters' upbringing?

4 Ramona's lack of a father figure no doubt influenced her choice of male companions in adult life. Does this explain her ambivalent attitude toward men? How did Tyrone and his father, Perry, fulfill Ramona's image of, and need for, men in her life?

5 What made Mae's treatment of her daughter change so drastically after the murder of Donald Booker? Do you think Ramona's forgiveness at the end of the book was plausible after a lifetime of neglect and abuse?

6 Much of the story takes place during the Civil Rights Movement. Discuss the paradoxical impact of the Civil Rights Act and its effect on Clarise, Finch, and their family.

7 Ramona has been described by the author as the book's central character. In what ways is she more fully developed than Clarise or Mae? How does she benefit by perpetuating her conflicting nature?

THIS BODY

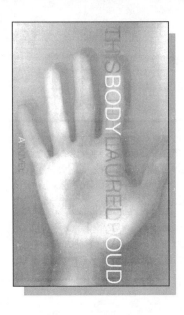

Author: Laurel Doud

Publisher: Back Bay Books
(Little, Brown & Co.), 1998

Website: www.littlebrown.com

Available in:
Hardcover, 272 pages. $23.95
(ISBN 0-316-19675-4)

Genre: Fiction

Summary

Katharine Ashley, dutiful wife and mother of two teenagers, dies in her sleep and wakes up one year later on the floor of a strange bathroom in a strange city—in a stranger's body. Thisby Bennet's lovely body, however, also has a heroin addiction, an abusive boyfriend, and a family that has been disappointed and alienated for years. Finding herself unable to go home—her husband has, horrifyingly, remarried—Katharine lets her mothering instincts take over. She comes to understand that she has much in common with this new body and that in order to be whole again, she must redeem not only Thisby's complicated past but also her own.

Recommended by: *Entertainment Weekly*

"[Doud's] frisky, riveting debut...proves equally engrossing for the senses, soul, and mind. Grade: A"

Author Biography

Laurel Doud is a research librarian who lives with her family in San Jose, California. This is her first novel.

Topics to Consider

1   The Katharine/Thisby character is obviously fictional, but somehow easily believable. If you were to find yourself awakening as someone else tomorrow morning, what kind of person would you want to try on? Appreciate the family that comes with it, as for Katharine this is her biggest struggle.

2   What a rare opportunity at insight Katharine is afforded: to be given a second chance at life, to be younger. She has a hard time seeing it as an opportunity. In fact, she mostly sees her situation as a predicament. But how does Katharine use this mind/body switch to her advantage?

3   The book is a constant struggle between the responsibilities of parenthood and the recklessness of youth. Much of Katharine's dialogue with herself addresses these issues in great detail. How have you realized a new appreciation for one or the other?

4   It could probably be said that the only time Katharine easily embraces Thisby's lifestyle is in her sexual encounters. In every other situation the Katharine/Thisby character is controlled by Katharine. Clearly the body plays a large role in one's sexual tendencies, but is the author trying to tell us that these sexual tendencies are *driven* by the body, not the mind? If so, do you agree or disagree?

5   Discuss Katharine's family and the Bennett family. Although they're from very different backgrounds, what similarities do they share?

THE TREE OF RED STARS

Author: Tessa Bridal
Publisher: Milkweed Editions, 1997
Website: www.milkweed.org
Available in:
Paperback, 294 pages. $13.95
(ISBN 1-57131-023-1)
Genre: Fiction

Summary

Winner of the Milkweed Prize for Fiction, this novel—set in Uruguay—begins quietly and takes the reader by storm, in much the same way that the violence of her country's dictatorship overtakes the main character, Magda. The daughter of an upper middle-class family in Montevideo, Magda must choose whether to support her friends, who have become insurgents, or her family and country's corroding power structure. The novel is at once a compelling love story and the moving portrait of a family, a neighborhood, and a country. It recounts political tragedy with compassion, but not melodrama. Issues of class, race, and ethnicity are dealt with subtly but powerfully.

Recommended by: *New York Times Book Review*

"Tessa Bridal brings a fresh voice to Latin American literature...She recounts Magda's perilous activities with a chillingly understated sense of inevitability."

Author Biography

Tessa Bridal, who now lives and works in Minnesota, spent the first half of her life in Uruguay and Brazil. She also has lived in Washington, D.C., and London. She vividly recalls the unrest of Uruguay in the 1970s, when no one was left untouched by the violence. In this book, she tells the story of those who fought, but did not win, whose voices would otherwise be lost.

Topics to Consider

1   Compare the characters of Magda, Emilia, and Cora. What role did their backgrounds and family situations play in shaping their political beliefs and actions? How much do friendships determine one's political sympathies?

2   Although small, Uruguay's population (3 million people) is comprised of many different ethnic groups, including European and Indian. How does the author convey this mosaic in her novel? Do you think this blend strengthens or weakens the country in times of crisis?

3   What was the role of the United States in Latin America during the cold war? How often do Americans see or understand the impact of US actions on the lives, loves and friendships of people abroad?

4   Have you experienced a situation in which your personal beliefs have come between you and your friends and family? Or in which your children, parents, or siblings have broken away because of a matter of belief or conviction? Can you imagine, in this country, a climate in which these divided loyalties threaten your personal safety?

5   What do you think of the ways Americans and America are depicted in this novel? Is it accurate? If Magda's story were taking place now, how would it be different?

6   How was Magda's life changed by her visit to the United States?

7   Marco is depicted as a man who loves his country enough to join the military, and yet also is condemned as a traitor. Wouldn't it have been easier for him to leave his military service? Why would he choose to put himself in the precarious position of undermining the very authority to which he pledged allegiance?

TRESPASSING

Author: Gwendolyn M. Parker

Publisher: Mariner Books, 1997

Available in:
Quality paperback, 210 pages. $11.00
(ISBN 0-395-92620-3)

Genre: Memoir/
African American/Business

Summary

For every woman who has found herself an outcast in the business world, *Trespassing* is a deeply moving and cautionary tale. With candor and dignity, Gwendolyn M. Parker recounts her perilous journey through some of the most exclusive institutions in America. This is the story of a woman who did everything right—the finest schools, a fast-track career on Wall Street—and yet no matter her talent and accomplishments, she discovered that sexism and racism still prevail at the top.

Recommended by: New York Times Book Review

"The stings and isolation of a career at the top ... Engagingly written and fluidly paced."

Author Biography

Gwendolyn M. Parker is the author of the novel *These Same Long Bones.* She left her career as an international tax attorney and marketing manager on Wall Street in order to write. Born in North Carolina, she now lives in Connecticut.

Topics to Consider

1   Community is very important to Gwen. Which communities does she strive to join? Where does she ultimately find acceptance and a true sense of community? How does the desire to fit in and be accepted influence her? What defines community for you? Where do you place yourself in that community?

2   How does she find the courage to break away from what is expected and be herself—doing what is right for her?

3   Gwen's life is marked by a sense of dislocation (moving from the north to the south, small town to big city, being black in a white world, etc.). How does she handle this and what does she learn about herself in the process?

4   Much of Gwen's motivation seems to come from a place of burden. She feels compelled to push open doors and establish a place for others of her race and gender to follow. How does this feeling of "racial avenger" manifest itself? To what extent does this influence her decision-making process? Have you ever found yourself in a position to affect change for others of your class/race/gender? How did this make you feel?

5   Gwen experiences, first hand, the differences between the black world in the south (her sheltered and privileged life in Durham) and the black world in the north. How is she made aware of these differences? How does the family's northern lifestyle change her parents?

6   Most of what Gwen comes to understand about cliques, race and class distinction she learns from "trespassing" in the halls of privilege. Have you ever been in a position to trespass—to show up in places where people, either because of assumed stereotypes or ignorance, least expect you? What did you learn from such an experience? What does Gwen learn?

7   What triggers her departure from American Express? Why is she finally able to break loose from what is expected of her? What is it that finally captures her allegiance?

"Marvelously vivid ... a quietly audacious book."
—*The New York Times Book Review*

The **Truest** **Pleasure**

A Novel

ROBERT MORGAN

THE TRUEST PLEASURE

Author: Robert Morgan

Publisher: Algonquin Books of Chapel Hill, 1998

Website: www.algonquin.com

Available in: Paperback, 336 pages. $11.95 (ISBN 1-56512-222-4)

Genre: Fiction

Summary

Ginny and Tom have a practical marriage. Tom wants land to call his own, and Ginny knows she can't manage her aging father's farm by herself. They enjoy a mutual attraction that sometimes grows into a deeply gratifying love, but their obsessions always, inevitably, end up in the way. Tom's obsession is easy to understand. He's a workaholic who hoards time and money. Ginny's is less predictable. That she loses control of her dignity, that she speaks in tongues, that she is "saved," seem to her a blessing and to Tom a disgrace. It's not until Tom lies at the mercy of a disease for which the mountain doctor has no cure that Ginny realizes her truest pleasure.

Recommended by: *The Washington Post Book World*

"Morgan's simple, eloquent language grounds the story in a tough farm life, his language pulses with poetry."

Author Biography

Robert Morgan, a native of the Carolina Blue Ridge Mountains, was raised on land settled by his Welsh ancestors. He is the author of nine volumes of poetry and three previous books of fiction and is the recipient of several fellowships. He is a professor of English at Cornell University.

Topics to Consider

1 Ginny has an almost mystical view of nature while Tom is thoroughly grounded in the literal, physical reality of the world around him. What is it that attracts these two? Do you believe that opposites attract?

2 Tom longs for land to call his own. What does land mean to him? Why is land ownership so significant to generations of other Americans?

3 Compare Tom's feeling about work to Ginny's feelings about religion. How are they similar?

4 In Ginny's experience, is there common ground between religion and sex? If so, what is it? Is her notion blasphemous?

5 This story is set in a time and place where diseases like cholera, pneumonia, or typhoid fever are ever threatening. How might your life be different if you knew you could be struck down at any moment by disease? How do Ginny and Tom face disease?

6 Does Ginny have reason to be jealous of Florrie? How is Florrie different from Ginny?

7 In the rural Appalachian world of Ginny and Tom, the daily work of living occupies much of their time. Are our modern lives similarly occupied? How are they similar, and how are they different? Is this a sign of progress? Is it an improvement?

8 In her letter to Locke, Ginny describes her rapidly shifting moods. Is there a positive aspect of her blue periods? When is Ginny most creative? When are you most creative?

9 Ginny says that "...a woman naturally comes to think like her husband sometimes." Do you believe this? Is Ginny what you would call "an independent woman"?

10 To what do you attribute the bitterness and fighting between Tom and Ginny? Is one more to blame than the other?

11 What was Ginny's truest pleasure? What was Tom's?

TUESDAYS WITH MORRIE
An Old Man, A Young Man, and Life's Greatest Lessons

Author: Mitch Albom

Publisher: Doubleday, 1997

Website:
www.tuesdayswithmorrie.com

Available in:
Hardcover, 192 pages. $19.95
(ISBN 0-385-48451-8)

Genre: Nonfiction/Inspiration

Summary

A *New York Times* bestseller for more than one year, with more than one million copies in print, *Tuesdays with Morrie* is a moving celebration of life. Author **Mitch Albom** chronicles his time spent with a beloved college professor, Morrie Schwartz. Morrie's refreshing outlook on life—and his own imminent death—is expressed beautifully and simply and serves as a powerful reminder of what's really important in life.

Recommended by: Bernie S. Siegel, M.D.

"This book is an incredible treasure. One's sense of our mortality is a great teacher and source of enlightenment. To have a teacher share this experience provides us with profound wisdom and insight. I laughed, cried and ordered five copies for our children."

Author Biography

Mitch Albom writes for the *Detroit Free Press*, and has been voted America's No. 1 sports columnist ten times by the Associated Press Sports Editors. A former professional musician, Albom hosts a daily radio show on WJR in Detroit and appears regularly on ESPN's "The Sports Reporters." He is the author of *Bo* and *Fab Five*, both national bestsellers. He lives with his wife, Janine, in Michigan.

Topics to Consider

1 Who do you think got more out of their Tuesday meetings, Mitch or Morrie? In what ways? How do you think each would answer this question?

2 Would Mitch have listened if Morrie hadn't been dying? Does impending death automatically make one's voice able to penetrate where it couldn't before?

3 Most of us have read of people discussing the way they'd like to die, or, perhaps, have been a part of that conversation. Has reading this book changed your opinion?

4 On *Nightline*, Morrie spoke to Ted Koppel of the pain he still felt about his mother's death seventy years prior to the interview. Is your experience with loss similar or different?

5 How might have Morrie reacted if he'd contracted ALS when he was Mitch's age?

6 Talk about the role of meaningful coincidence, synchronicity, in the book and in Mitch and Morrie's friendship.

7 Morrie said, "If you've found meaning in your life, you don't want to go back. You want to go forward." (p. 118) Is this true in your experience?

8 As his visits with Morrie continued, Mitch explored some other cultures and religions and how each views death. Discuss these and any others that you've studied.

9 Morrie shares his opinions about having children (p.93) and about marriage (p. 149). In what ways do you agree or disagree?

10 Discuss the practical side of Morrie's advice: "Only an open heart will allow you to float equally between everyone." (p.128) How could this advice be useful the next time you're in a social or other situation where you feel out of place or uncomfortable?

11 Would Morrie's lessons have carried less weight if Mitch and Peter hadn't resumed contact by book's end?

Editor's note: Additional topics for discussion may be found at www.tuesdayswithmorrie.com.

TURNIP BLUES

Author: Helen Campbell

Publisher: Spinsters Ink, 1998

Website: www.spinsters-ink.com

Available in:
Paperback, 256 pages. $10.95
(ISBN 1-883523-23-0)

Genre: Fiction

Summary

The enduring story of the journey of a lifetime for two 75-year-old women—Mrs. Kuzo and Mrs. Lemack. As the two drive across Pennsylvania to visit the grave of legendary blues singer Bessie Smith, Mrs. Kuzo reflects upon her own life's journey, growing up in a dysfunctional immigrant family in Depression-era Pittsburgh. As Mrs. Kuzo and Mrs. Lemack reach their journey's end in Philadelphia, Mrs. Kuzo arrives at her own destination, learning an important truth that recasts her entire life.

Recommended by: Sandra Martz, editor, *When I am an Old Woman, I Shall Wear Purple*

*"**Turnip Blues** shines its light on the lives of two gritty old women whose indomitable spirits carry them through the hardships of their 'outsider' status as members of poor, immigrant families. This is a book that takes us into the hearts of two women who remind us what **America** is really all about!"*

Author Biography

Helen Campbell lives in Germany, where she teaches for the University of Maryland European Division. Ms. Campbell was awarded a 1997 Fiction Fellowship from the Pennsylvania Council on the Arts. *Turnip Blues* is her first novel.

Topics to Consider

1 Mrs. Lemack says, "The way I see things, Mrs. Kuzo, family's just a state of mind. The real families are the ones you pick." Do you agree with Mrs. Lemack? How do you define family?

2 Why does Mrs. Lemack want to be part of Bessie Smith's family? What does it mean for her to be so identified with a celebrity?

3 Do you believe that a bird really collided with Mrs. Kuzo's car? Whether it did or not, what does the bird represent for Mrs. Kuzo?

4 Since childhood, Mrs. Kuzo has blamed herself for her sister Lily's death. Did (or do) you hold yourself responsible for childhood events over which you had no control?

5 Mrs. Lemack tells Mrs. Kuzo she's not to blame for her children's failures in life, while Vicky argues that parents are responsible for who their children become. With whom do you agree?

6 From childhood on, Mrs. Kuzo is plagued with concerns about her family's reputation. How much of this concern is related to the immigrant status of the family? What does this say about the way immigrants are viewed and/or treated in the United States?

7 What does Mrs. Kuzo mean when she says that "men alone can't ruin women's lives" after she learns the truth about Annie?

8 Vicky says life is a lottery. Is it?

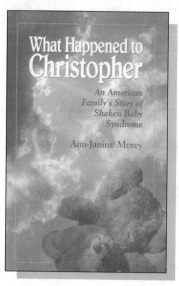

WHAT HAPPENED TO CHRISTOPHER
An American Family's Story of Shaken Baby Syndrome

Author: Ann-Janine Morey

Publisher: Southern Illinois University Press, 1998

Website: www.siu.edu/~siupress/titles/f98_titles/morey_what.htm

Available in: Hardcover, 195 pages. $22.95 (ISBN 0-8093-2215-3)

Genre: Nonfiction/Family/Parenting

Summary

As an alternate juror in a 1995 trial in Murphysboro, Illinois, Ann-Janine Morey witnessed the court proceedings in a case against a live-in boyfriend who fatally shook a nineteen-month-old baby. This book memorializes the short life of Christopher Attig, showing what Christopher meant to those closest to him. Morey conducted extensive interviews with the child's parents and grandparents, as well as officials involved in the case. By presenting the accumulated findings relative to Shaken Baby Syndrome, Morey seeks through education to help prevent future deaths like Christopher's.

Recommended by: Alvin Poussaint, MD, *Harvard Med. School*

"This book details the events leading up to SBS and will serve as a valuable resource for the prevention of such tragedies. I recommend it to all parents and caregivers."

Author Biography

Ann-Janine Morey is a professor of English at Southern Illinois University at Carbondale. She is the author of ***Apples and Ashes: Culture, Metaphor and Morality in the American Dream*** and ***Religion and Sexuality in American Literature.***

Topics to Consider

1 Discuss your impressions of Christopher's family, and any differences and similarities to your own.

2 Is there such a thing as a "typical" perpetrator in Shaken Baby Syndrome cases?

3 If you had been a member of the jury in this case, how would you feel about the evidence presented?

4 What are some of the circumstances that can contribute to shaking a baby?

5 If you were able to interview the perpetrator of this crime, what would you most want to know? What would you most want to say to him?

6 What can family members do to better cope with the loss of a child?

7 How does Christopher's story compare to that of the recent "nanny" case in Massachusetts?

8 What can be done to prevent Shaken Baby Syndrome?

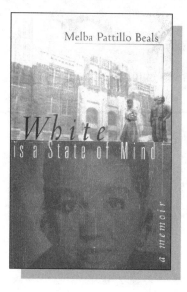

WHITE IS A STATE OF MIND

Author: Melba Pattillo Beals

Publisher: G. P. Putnam's Sons, 1999

Website: www.penguinputnam.com

Available in:
Hardcover, 304 pages. $23.95
(ISBN 0-399-14464-1)

Genre: Nonfiction/Memoir

Summary

Beals' first book, **Warriors Don't Cry**, told the story of her pivotal role in civil rights history as one of the "Little Rock Nine," who desegregated Central High School. In this follow-up memoir, Beals looks at the healing journey she has taken. She reflects on the white California family who opened their home and heart to her after her traumatic experiences in the South, and the slow but rewarding voyage toward forgiveness and compassion that culminated in a successful career and a new outlook on life. With an utterly unique story to tell, Beals offers a tale of the true heart of America—where "freedom is a state of mind."

Author Biography

Melba Pattillo Beals is the author of the critically acclaimed **Warriors Don't Cry** and has recently been awarded a Congressional Gold Medal for her part in the civil rights movement. She has written numerous articles for such periodicals as *People, Essence,* and the *San Francisco Examiner.* Her bestselling primer on public relations, **Expose Yourself: Using the Power of Public Relations to Promote Your Business and Yourself,** is an acknowledged industry reference. Melba lives in Northern California with her two sons.

Topics to Consider

1   Beals returns to the south from a summer of "star" treatment in the north. Have you ever been given the opportunity to escape the reality of your circumstances for a short period of time? What influence does this 'escape' have when you return to the reality of your situation? How does Melba deal with this?

2   Melba's travels into more secure environments give her a glimpse of her potential—what might await her if she only has the nerve and/or motivation to go for it. When she is thrust back into an area of limitation brought on by danger/fear (in the form of verbal/physical attacks), does she lose sight of her goals and what she perceives as her fate? How does this "nightmare beneath the surface" unnerve her? What does she do about it?

3   Discovering that "white is a state of mind" is a major epiphany for Melba. What triggers this understanding and how does she learn to use it to her advantage? Have you ever experienced a clarifying moment such as this?

4   Melba's involvement in the Civil rights movement as a high school student forces her to make a number of personal sacrifices. Discuss what, if anything, is to be gained by making personal sacrifices for the greater good?

5   How does Melba's religion guide and inspire her? How important is her faith? Does this faith come from within or is it directed by what her mother and grandmother expect of her? Do you view faith and religion as one and the same or separately?

6   What is significant about her relationship with Matt? In what ways can Melba's biracial child stand as a metaphor for her life?

7   Melba struggles with feeling cast out by both black and white communities. How does she attempt to fit in? How does she alter her state of mind from one of imprisonment to one of being set free? After all that she has experienced, where does she finally find the strength to transcend her circumstances and succeed?

WOMAN
An Intimate Geography

Author: Natalie Angier

Publisher: Houghton Mifflin, 1999

Website: www.hmco.com

Available in:
Hardcover, 416 pages. $25.00
(ISBN 0-395-69130-3)

Genre: Nonfiction/Women's Studies/
Science and Biology

Summary

Natalie Angier lifts the veil of secrecy from that most enigmatic of evolutionary masterpieces, the female body, exploring the essence of what it means to be a woman. Angier takes on everything from organs (breasts "are funny things, really, and we should learn to laugh at them") to orgasm (happily for women, the clitoris has 8,000 nerve fibers, twice the number in the penis). As she also dives into hot topics such as menopause exercise, and evolutionary psychologists' faddish views of "female nature," she creates a joyful, fresh vision of womanhood.

Recommended by: *Dr. Susan Love*

*"In **Woman**, Natalie Angier wields her poetic scalpel to explore female biology, and the result is awesome."*

Author Biography

Natalie Angier writes about biology for the *New York Times*, where she has won a Pulitzer Prize and other awards. Her previous books, which have received wide acclaim, are ***The Beauty of the Beastly*** and ***Natural Obsessions***, both available from Mariner Books.

Topics to Consider

1   Natalie Angier says that this book sets out to tackle the question, "What makes a woman?" What answers does she offer?

2   Were you surprised by any of the information presented? Were there any issues you had not thought about before?

3   Which of the author's humorous takes do you most enjoy?

4   Which of Angier's pointed commentary affects you most strongly, and how?

5   Angier makes frequent comparisons between humans and other mammals. In what cases do you find these analogies most instructive?

6   What elements does Angier seem to consider the most impressive in a woman's "intimate geography?" What parts of that discussion most intrigue you?

7   After reading this book, when do you think anatomy determines a woman's behavior and when can a woman manipulate or exploit her anatomy?

8   Natalie Angier is a reporter, not a scientist or medical doctor. Does this fact affect your acceptance of her work? If so, why?

9   Angier writes that women live "in a state of permanent revolution." What do you think she means?

10 The author has a daughter who is too young to realize what it means to be female. While Angier contends that "maybe it should mean nothing," do you find this statement consistent with the book's thesis?

A WOMAN DETERMINED

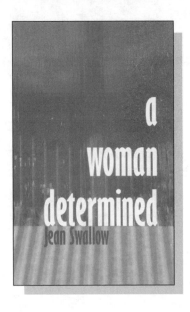

Author: Jean Swallow

Publisher: Spinsters Ink, 1998

Website: www.spinsters-ink.com

Available in:
Paperback, 264 pages. $10.95
(ISBN 1-883523-28-1)

Genre: Fiction

Summary

The multi-layered story of how an automobile accident profoundly transforms the lives of two women, Margaret Donovan, the victim, and her attorney, Laura Gilbert. In parallel narratives, the two women recall their search for justice, and, in the process, tell the story of a close-knit lesbian community and the consequences of crises upon that community, its members, and its institutions. This novel explores women's relationships, how women tend to hold each other to impossibly high standards, and the subsequent anger directed towards those women who fail to meet others' expectations. Ultimately, this is a story of hope—of how two women reach deep within themselves to find the truths of their lives, the reality they can and need to embrace.

Recommended by: Traci Vogel, *The Stranger* (Seattle, WA)

"Swallow's book is not only full of literary suspense but depicts believable characters in very complicated situations."

Author Biography

Jean Swallow is the author of *Leave a Light On for Me*, editor of two anthologies, *Out From Under: Sober Dykes and Our Friends* and *The Next Step*, and collaborator on a book of photos and interviews, *Making Love Visible: In Celebration of Gay & Lesbian Families*. Jean Swallow committed suicide in 1995 at age 42.

Topics to Consider

1   Explain the significance of the title, *A Woman Determined*. Who is she and what is she determined to do?

2   Do you think the relationship between Margaret and Laura would have been different if Laura had been a man? If so, how?

3   Do you think that women indeed do hold each other up to impossibly high standards? Why or why not?

4   Margaret and Laura view the same situations very differently. Is one woman right and the other wrong? Can they both be right?

5   If Margaret and Laura were your friends, would you tend to believe one over the other? Why?

6   Has reading *A Woman Determined* changed your views on universal health care? Why or why not?

7   Examine Dr. Lennox's relationship with Duke's little girl. How do you think Margaret would feel if she knew he cared about her the way he obviously does?

8   Why do you suppose Margaret calls her father Duke instead of "father," "dad," or the like?

9   Margaret considers weight to be a tool of the patriarchy to oppress women. Do you agree or disagree with Margaret?

10 Do you think Margaret would have received a larger settlement if she were thinner? Why or why not?

11 Do you think that Margaret and Laura attain resolution? How or why not?

YOUR BLUE-EYED BOY

Author: Helen Dunmore

Publisher: Little, Brown & Co., 1998

Website: www.littlebrown.com

Available in:
Hardcover, 282 pages. $23.95
(ISBN 0-316-19738-6)

Genre: Fiction

Summary

Simone is thirty-eight, a district judge whose husband, Donald, is on the verge of bankruptcy and breakdown. Each morning she leaves him with their two young boys while she drives to court to assess evidence and pass judgment. In her public life she must "make sense of things that really don't make sense at all." In her private life she struggles to control chaos and mounting debt, with only an early-morning swim to keep her sane. One such morning a letter arrives, addressed to Simone and postmarked New York. Someone she has tried to forget has not forgotten her. Simone's private history is about to collide with her public world.

Recommended by: Mark Lindquist, *NY Times Book Review*

"A meditation on the past and loss and how we cope with who we become...Dunmore writes gracefully and has an excellent sense of place."

Author Biography

Helen Dunmore, winner of Britain's first-ever Orange Prize, for the year's best novel by a woman, is a writer of novels, short stories, and poetry. She lives in Bristol, England, with her husband and children.

Topics to Consider

1 Do you agree with Simone's belief, regarding TV and children in particular since Vietnam, that "it is wrong to see so much and understand so little"? (p. 11) If so, how could this be changed?

2 The novel is full of surprises, in terms of both character and event. Discuss how this is achieved and the effect it has on the reader.

3 Discuss the ways in which Donald, Simone and their children cope with Donald's bankruptcy and Simone's financial support of the family. How do you imagine you would cope in similar circumstances?

4 How does history impact certain characters—Michael and Simone, for example—and how does their response to it express their individual selves?

5 Confronting Simone's fears during the squall, Michael says that the worst thing that could happen is "We could drown." (p. 122) What is the worst that could happen to Simone if the truth of her past were to surface? Is she right to fear it?

6 Is Michael correct in saying, "You can't pretend the past didn't happen"? (p. 145) What truths do the pictures reveal to Simone, not only about the past but also about her present with Donald and the children?

7 Michael questions Simone's abilities to be a judge of others. Do you agree with his assessment? To be a good judge, is it necessary to be impartial?

8 Can victims of blackmail ever be said to be at least partially to blame for what happens to them?

9 How else might Simone have reacted to Michael falling off the seawall, and what do you imagine the outcome would have been?

SPECIAL OFFER

Add something new and exciting
to your next meeting
by including the author
in your discussion

For 1100 years men have denied her existence. She is the legend that will not die—
Pope Joan, the first and only woman ever to
sit on the throne of St. Peter. This stirring
novel, based on historical record, brings
the Dark Ages to life in all their brutal
splendor and shares the dramatic story of
an unforgettable woman, reminiscent of
Jane Austen's Emma, Jean Auel's Ayla, and
other heroines who struggle against restric-
tions their souls will not accept.

Donna Woolfolk Cross, author of the international bestseller *Pope Joan*, will chat by telephone with book discussion
groups. This special offer has been made in conjunction with
the launch of Ballantine's new Reader's Circle Books, designed
specifically for reading groups. Every copy of *Pope Joan* has
discussion questions, an interview with the author, and provocative reviews bound right into the back of the book itself.

Interested reading groups can leave a message on the guest-
book of the *Pope Joan* website (*www.popejoan.com*) or at
315-469-2615, and the author will contact them to set up a
mutually convenient time for a chat. Or they can fax the author
directly at 315-469-1680.

Pope Joan

Ballantine Books, 1997
Paperback, 422 pages, $12.95
ISBN 0-345-41626-0

NEW TITLES

At your
bookstore, or call
1-800-227-2872
wjk@ctr.pcusa.org

WESTMINSTER
JOHN KNOX PRESS
100 Witherspoon Street
Louisville, KY 40202-1396

ATHENA'S DISGUISES
Mentors In Everyday Life

Susan Ford Wiltshire

A wise and perceptive book
that explores the multitude
of ways mentoring occurs
in our lives: through
contacts with friends,
family, children, elders,
artists, community
peacemakers—even chance
encounters with strangers.
Using inspiring examples of
several remarkable women
who touched her own life,
Wiltshire shows that
mentors are often not
recognized at first, and in
some cases, not until many
years after their
contributions are made.

Cloth • $19.00 • 149 pp
ISBN 0-664-22101-7

RESOURCES

The Internet

Reading Group Choices Online – Includes a directory of over 550 guides available from publishers as well as more than 150 guides that can be printed directly from the site.
www.readinggroupchoices.com

Publisher Web Sites:
Avon—
www.AvonBooks.com/avon/fiction/guides.html
Doubleday—
www.bdd.com/read
HarperCollins—
www.harpercollins.com/readers/index.htm
Penguin Putnam—
www.penguinputnam.com/clubppi/index.htm
Random House/Ballantine—
www.randomhouse.com/BB/readerscircle/index.html
Random House/Vintage—
www.randomhouse.com/vintage/read
Simon & Schuster—
www.SimonSays.com/reading/guides

Newsletters

Reverberations News Journal, Rachel Jacobsohn's publication of the Association of Book Group Readers and Leaders. Annual membership including subscription is $18. Contact:
ABGRL
Box 885
Highland Park, IL 60035
(847) 266-0431
E-mail: *rachelj@interaccess.com*

Book Lovers, quarterly book review publication with recommendations by the editor and librarians. Annual subscription is $10. Contact:
Book Lovers
PO Box 511396
Milwaukee, WI 53203-0241
414/384-2300
www.execpc.com/~booklove

Newsletters (continued)

Booknews and Views, quarterly newsletter of Books, Etcetera. Annual subscription is $10. Contact:

Books, Etcetera
228 Commercial Street #1957
Nevada City, CA 95959
(530) 478-9400

A Friend Who Reads, bimonthly newsletter that's perfect for avid readers. Annual subscription is $12. Contact:

Creekside Press
1235 Wildwood Road
Boulder, CO 80303
(303) 499-9207

Books & Journals

Circles of Sisterhood: A Book Discussion Group Guide for Women of Color by Pat Neblett.
Published by Writers & Readers, ISBN 0-8631-6245-2, $14.

Family Book Sharing Groups: Start One in Your Neighborhood! by Marjorie Simic and Eleanor MacFarlane.
Published by Grayson Bernard Publishers, ISBN 1-8837-9011-5, $6.95.

Minnesota Women's Press Great Books. Contact:

Minnesota Women's Press
771 Raymond Avenue,
Saint Paul, MN 55114
(612) 646-3968

The Mother-Daughter Book Club: How Ten Busy Mothers and Daughters Came Together to Talk, Laugh and Learn Through Their Love of Reading by Shireen Dodson and Teresa Barker.
Published by HarperCollins, ISBN 0-0609-5242-3, $12.95.

The Reading Group Handbook: Everything You Need to Know from Choosing Members to Leading Discussions by Rachel W. Jacobsohn. Revised Edition.
Published by Hyperion, ISBN 0-7868-8324-3, $11.95.

Books & Journals (continued)

What to Read: The Essential Guide for Reading Group Members and Other Book Lovers by Mickey Pearlman. Published by HarperCollins, ISBN 0-0609-5061-7, $11.00.

The Reader's Companion published by Creekside Press. Available in black or burgundy leather-like binder, $19.95. Call (303) 499-9207.

A Reader's Journal published by Margie Adler, The Write Style. Available in six different designs, $9.95. Call (612) 928-1962.

A Young Reader's Journal:
A Lively Collection of Books and Ideas by Margie Adler The Write Style, $12.95. Call (612) 928-1962.

1999

JANUARY
S	M	T	W	T	F	S
					[1]	2
[3]	4	5	6	7	[8]	9
10	11	12	13	14	15	16
17	[18]	19	20	21	22	23
24	25	26	27	28	29	30
31						

FEBRUARY
S	M	T	W	T	F	S
	1	2	3	4	5	6
7	8	9	10	11	[12]	13
[14]	[15]	16	[17]	18	19	20
21	[22]	23	24	25	26	27
28						

MARCH
S	M	T	W	T	F	S
	1	2	3	4	5	6
7	8	9	10	11	12	13
14	15	16	[17]	18	19	20
21	22	23	24	25	26	27
[28]	29	30	31			

APRIL
S	M	T	W	T	F	S
				[1]	[2]	3
[4]	5	6	7	8	9	10
[11]	12	13	14	15	16	17
18	[19]	20	[21]	22	23	24
25	26	27	28	29	30	

MAY
S	M	T	W	T	F	S
						1
2	3	4	5	6	7	8
[9]	10	11	12	13	14	15
16	17	18	19	20	21	22
23	24	25	26	27	28	29
30	[31]					

JUNE
S	M	T	W	T	F	S
		1	2	3	4	5
6	7	8	9	10	11	12
13	[14]	15	16	17	18	19
[20]	21	22	23	24	25	26
27	28	29	30			

JULY
S	M	T	W	T	F	S
				1	2	3
[4]	5	6	7	8	9	10
11	12	13	14	15	16	17
18	19	20	21	22	23	24
25	26	27	28	29	30	31

AUGUST
S	M	T	W	T	F	S
1	2	3	4	5	6	7
8	[9]	10	11	12	13	14
15	16	17	18	19	[20]	21
22	23	24	25	26	27	28
29	30	31				

SEPTEMBER
S	M	T	W	T	F	S
			1	2	3	4
5	[6]	7	8	9	10	[11]
12	13	14	15	16	17	18
19	[20]	21	22	23	24	25
26	27	28	29	30		

OCTOBER
S	M	T	W	T	F	S
					1	2
3	4	5	6	7	8	9
10	[11]	12	13	14	15	16
17	18	19	20	21	22	23
[24]	25	26	27	28	29	30
[31]						

NOVEMBER
S	M	T	W	T	F	S
	1	[2]	3	4	5	6
7	8	9	10	[11]	12	13
14	15	16	17	18	19	20
21	22	23	24	[25]	26	27
28	29	30				

DECEMBER
S	M	T	W	T	F	S
			1	2	3	[4]
5	6	7	8	9	10	11
12	13	14	15	16	17	18
19	20	21	22	23	24	[25]
26	27	28	29	30	31	

2000

JANUARY
S	M	T	W	T	F	S
						[1]
2	[3]	4	5	6	7	8
9	10	11	12	13	14	15
16	[17]	18	19	20	21	22
23	24	25	26	27	28	29
30	31					

FEBRUARY
S	M	T	W	T	F	S
		1	2	3	4	5
6	7	8	9	10	11	[12]
13	[14]	15	16	17	18	19
20	[21]	[22]	23	24	25	26
27	28	29				

MARCH
S	M	T	W	T	F	S
			1	2	3	
5	6	7	[8]	9	10	11
12	[13]	14	15	16	[17]	18
19	20	21	22	23	24	25
26	27	28	29	30	31	

APRIL
S	M	T	W	T	F	S
						1
2	3	4	5	6	7	8
9	10	11	12	13	14	15
[16]	[17]	18	19	[20]	[21]	22
[23]	24	25	[26]	27	28	29
[30]						

MAY
S	M	T	W	T	F	S
	1	2	3	4	5	6
7	8	9	10	11	12	13
[14]	15	16	17	18	19	20
21	22	23	24	25	26	27
28	[29]	30	31			

JUNE
S	M	T	W	T	F	S
				1	2	3
4	5	6	7	8	9	10
11	12	13	[14]	15	16	17
[18]	19	20	21	22	23	24
25	26	27	28	29	30	

JULY
S	M	T	W	T	F	S
						1
2	3	[4]	5	6	7	8
9	10	11	12	13	14	15
16	17	18	19	20	21	22
23	24	25	26	27	28	29
30	31					

AUGUST
S	M	T	W	T	F	S
		1	2	3	4	5
6	7	8	9	10	11	12
13	[14]	15	16	17	[18]	19
20	21	22	23	24	25	26
27	28	29	30	31		

SEPTEMBER
S	M	T	W	T	F	S
					1	2
3	[4]	5	6	7	8	9
10	11	12	13	14	15	16
17	18	19	20	21	22	23
24	25	26	27	28	29	[30]

OCTOBER
S	M	T	W	T	F	S
1	2	3	4	5	6	7
8	[9]	10	11	12	13	14
15	16	17	18	19	20	21
22	23	24	25	26	27	28
29	30	[31]				

NOVEMBER
S	M	T	W	T	F	S
			1	2	3	4
5	6	[7]	8	9	10	[11]
12	13	14	15	16	17	18
19	20	21	22	[23]	24	25
26	27	28	29	30		

DECEMBER
S	M	T	W	T	F	S
					1	2
3	4	5	6	7	8	9
10	11	12	13	14	15	16
17	18	19	20	21	[22]	23
24	[25]	26	27	28	29	30
31						

BOOK GROUP MEETING DATES

January   _____

February   _____

March   _____

April   _____

May   _____

June   _____

July   _____

August   _____

September   _____

October   _____

November   _____

December   _____

January   _____

February   _____

March   _____

BOOK GROUP MEMBERS

Name _____
    Day phone _____ Eve. phone _____

Name _____
    Day phone _____ Eve. phone _____

Name _____
    Day phone _____ Eve. phone _____

Name _____
    Day phone _____ Eve. phone _____

Name _____
    Day phone _____ Eve. phone _____

Name _____
    Day phone _____ Eve. phone _____

Name _____
    Day phone _____ Eve. phone _____

Name _____
    Day phone _____ Eve. phone _____

Name _____
    Day phone _____ Eve. phone _____

Name _____
    Day phone _____ Eve. phone _____

Name _____
    Day phone _____ Eve. phone _____

INDEX BY SUBJECT / INTEREST AREA

INDEX BY SUBJECT / INTEREST AREA

(continued)

INDEX BY AUTHOR

INDEX BY AUTHOR

(continued)

INDEX BY AUTHOR
(continued)

INDEX BY AUTHOR
(continued)

INDEX BY GENRE

Nonfiction

INDEX BY GENRE

Fiction

INDEX BY GENRE

Fiction (continued)

Women's National Book Association

WNBA is an organization that brings together women and men who value the written word. There are ten chapters, located in: Atlanta, Binghamton, Boston, Dallas, Detroit, Los Angeles, Nashville, New York, San Francisco, and Washington D.C.

Whether you're a book lover or a book professional, consider becoming a part of the WNBA network. Programs feature speakers who address topics such as community literacy, the impact of advancements in technology, and other changes in the publishing industry. Several chapters sponsor informal reading discussion groups.

To find out how to contact a chapter near you, or to learn how to start a new chapter, write or call:

WNBA
160 Fifth Avenue
New York, NY 10010
212/675-7805
bookbuzz.com/wnba.htm

About Paz & Associates

The mission of Paz & Associates is to serve the book community by empowering people and organizations with new skills and insights that significantly increase their ability to serve customers and patrons. We offer a variety of products and services to bookstores, publishers, libraries and other book-related organizations, including:

♦ consulting on marketing, human resources, design, merchandising, and business operations, including financial analysis and inventory selection and control

♦ consulting with prospective and current publishers on financial dynamics, marketing and promotion strategies, co-op policies, book packaging, and bookseller relations to maximize sell-through

♦ customized, up-to-date mailing lists

♦ the monthly newsletter *Independent Bookselling Today!*

♦ *The Reader's Edge* newsletter marketing program for bookstores and libraries

♦ *Opening a Bookstore: The Essential Planning Guide*

♦ *Retail Training Center for Bookstores* (opening in Summer, 1999)

♦ *The Training Guide to FrontLine Bookselling*

♦ *Exceptional FrontLine Bookselling: It's All About Service,* a 60 minute training video

♦ *Greeting Cards* with designs to celebrate books and reading

For more information, please visit our website at:
www.pazbookbiz.com

Or contact:

Paz & Associates
2106 Twentieth Avenue South
Nashville, TN 37212-4312

800/260-8605 — phone
615/298-2303 — phone
615/298-9864 — fax
dpaz@pazbookbiz.com — email

About *Reading Group Choices*

This publication, the fifth edition of *Reading Group Choices*, was developed and produced by Paz & Associates, whose mission is to join with publishers and bookstores to develop resources and skills that promote books and reading.

Books for potential inclusion are recommended by book group members, librarians, booksellers, and publishers. All submissions are then reviewed by an Advisory Group of book industry professionals, to ensure the "discussibility" of each title. Once a title is approved for inclusion, publishers are then asked to underwrite production costs, so that copies of *Reading Group Choices* can be distributed for the cost of shipping and handling alone.

Twenty thousand copies of *Reading Group Choices* are distributed annually to independent bookstores, libraries, and directly to book groups. Back issues are available in photocopy form, at $5.00 each. Titles from previous issues are also posted on our new website at *readinggroupchoices.com*.

For additional copies of this publication, please call your local library or independent bookstore, or you may contact us at the address and phone number below. We will be happy to ship copies to you directly, or let you know of a bookstore in your area that has obtained copies of *Reading Group Choices*. Please be advised, however, that some bookstores will offer copies free of charge as a customer service, while others may charge the single-copy price of $4.95 each. Quantities are limited.

For more information, please visit our website at:
www.readinggroupchoices.com

Or contact:

Paz & Associates
2106 Twentieth Avenue South
Nashville, TN 37212-4312

800/260-8605 — phone
615/298-2303 — phone
615/298-9864 — fax
dpaz@pazbookbiz.com — email

Now online . . .

Your #1 Internet Resource
for Book Groups

www.readinggroupchoices.com

Looking for other great book selections for your book group? Want to know if guides are available for titles you have in mind? Want the latest scoop on newly released discussible books?

LOOK WHAT'S NEW	See what publishers have in store; get the inside scoop on new discussible books.
DIRECTORY OF AVAILABLE GUIDES	Search a comprehensive list of over 550 titles with discussion guides—print more than 150 directly from the site.
TIPS ON STARTING A BOOK GROUP	Thinking about starting a book group? Here are some quick tips and ideas to get you going.
GUIDANCE FOR GROUP LEADERS	Expert advice on running a successful book discussion group.
PAST EDITIONS	Past editions of *Reading Group Choices* you can browse and download.

For resources ready for you to use on the world-wide web, visit
www.readinggroupchoices.com